new   21 -

W9-CUP-228

Sitting Shiva on Minto Avenue, by Toots

Erín Moure

Sitting Shiva on Minto Avenue,

by Toots

New Star Books
Vancouver | 2017

I'm not sure if the people, places, or events depicted in this memoir resemble anyone or anything living or dead. They are my memories, and memory is a work of the imagination.

NEW STAR BOOKS LTD.
107–3477 Commercial Street, Vancouver, BC V5N 4E8   CANADA
1574 Gulf Road, No. 1517, Point Roberts, WA 98281   USA
www.NewStarBooks.com   info@NewStarBooks.com

Copyright Erín Moure 2017. All rights reserved. No part of this work may be reproduced, stored in a retrieval system or transmitted, in any form or by any means, without the prior written consent of the publisher or a licence from Access Copyright.

The publisher acknowledges the financial support of the Canada Council for the Arts and the British Columbia Arts Council.

Cataloguing information for this book is available from Library and Archives Canada, www.collectionscanada.gc.ca.

Cover design: Oliver McPartlin / mcpartlin.ca
Cover image: detail from "Ovaltine Café" by Greg Girard, used by permission
Image on pages 90 and 126 (bottom) from *Pierrot à Montréal* copyright 1957 National Film Board of Canada. All rights reserved.
Printed on 100% post-consumer recycled paper
Printed and bound in Canada by Imprimerie Gauvin
First printing, October 2017

In memory of

Paul Émile Savard

28 September 1943 — 4 December 2015

Whose lives are already considered not lives, or only partially living, or already dead and gone, prior to any explicit destruction or abandonment? Of course, this question becomes more acute for someone, anyone, who already understands him- or herself to be a dispensable sort of being, one who registers at an affective and corporeal level that his or her life is not worth safeguarding, protecting, and valuing. This is someone who understands that she or he will not be grieved if his or her life is lost, and so one for whom the conditional claim "I would not be grieved" is actively lived in the present moment. If it turns out that I have no certainty that I will have food or shelter, or that no social network or institution would catch me if I fall, then I come to belong to the ungrievable. This does not mean that there won't be some who grieve me . . .

Judith Butler, *Notes Toward a Performative Theory of Assembly*

Il y a ici la conscience inavouée que l'élément authen-
tiquement politique consiste précisément en cette
clandestinité incommunicable, presque ridicule, de la
vie privée. En effet, il est certain que la vie clandestine,
notre *forme-de-vie*, est chose si intime et si proche que,
si nous tentons de la saisir, elle ne nous laisse entre les
mains que l'impénétrable, l'ennuyeuse quotidienneté.

Giorgio Agamben, *L'usage des corps*

There is here the unarticulated realization that what is truly
political consists precisely in the incommunicable, almost
ridiculous clandestinity of our private lives. In effect, it's certain
that this clandestine life, our *forme-de-vie*, is something so
intimate and so close to us that if we try to grasp it, all we hold
in our hands is the impenetrable dreariness of everyday.

Giorgio Agamben, *The Use of Bodies*

What I Knew About the Little Man

He was born in Québec in the Abitibi region on September 28, 1943. Or he was born in Montréal. I have a photo of him on a second-floor balcony with his mom when he was eight months old. In Montréal, in NDG. She has a beautiful dress in the photo and he is smiling.

His father and mother had been colonists in the Abitibi region under the *Plan de colonisation Vautrin*. The life was hard there under the iron hand of the Church and they returned to Montréal either before or after the little man was born. Paul Émile. Their eldest. Later they had two more, Hélène and Jean. Paul Émile, despite his own difficult life, outlived them all.

His father, Yvan or Yvon, had had a corner store in Montréal, or worked in one, before going north as a colonist. It was the Depression. The church was promoting the salvation of the French-Canadian people via a return to the land. The curés ruled all aspects of life there. The family, like others, returned to the city broke, everything lost to them, and his father became a coach cleaner for the CPR. It was a dignified, union job. His mother was a housewife.

I wonder about the word "was," the word "is." To use either of them is like pushing a sewing needle through heavy material. Hide, or canvas. My thumbs hurt.

Either his mother or his father was half Indigenous, half Wendat, or *Huron*, as he called it. He had an old photo of his grandmother in traditional clothing that he was very proud of, from the early twentieth century, and said she was a princess. All his life, though raised Catholic according to the imperative of the time, he practised a more reverent spirituality: god, he said, was breath, was air. We took in god when we breathed in, and we breathed god out again. All breathing animals did this; plants did this.

Then he would purse his lips and breathe out a little breath of wind.

I have another photo of him given me by his Mom, of him at the age of six in a little woollen suit and tie and he looked the same age as he was when I knew him.

Only once, in Vancouver where we lived together, was he ever in an alcohol treatment program for First Nations and Métis (he was in others, and often; of all of them he hated Alcoholics Anonymous the most). This was in the early '80s, but after we'd parted ways. Maybe it was the first time such a program had existed. He accepted the spirituality of the program but found it hard as the West Coast cultures were different, and he had been raised in white culture as a French-Canadian in Montréal.

He had a Grade 7 education, the highest level of public school education in French in his day. Yet he always read the newspaper and was cognizant of politics and sports, and liked to discuss them. He had had no chance for further education. The *collège classique* was not for those of his social class, unless a curé took them in hand. I was impressed by him as he was erudite, to me, and functionally literate, which was not always true for others in his class and position.

He never abided any prejudice. He defended both gay people (as he said, in the late '70s, in a just world it wouldn't make any difference if you were gay or straight) and First Nations people, and helped many old alcoholics living alone on skid row in the Downtown Eastside, visiting them, buying them groceries when he had a job. Like Postie, who lived in the skinny Hotel Empress, which had just a small neon sign, but its name painted huge on the west wall of the building. In those days, the '70s and early '80s, the Downtown Eastside was impoverished and was an area of prostitution, alcohol and drugs, but it was inhabited, lively. It wasn't the dead abandoned zone of later on.

We ate seafood at the Only.

Before I'd met him and before he'd had a steady job at CN as a waiter then steward, he'd had unemployed periods of bad alcoholism, and he had stories of the prostitutes and police, and of police mistreatment of the poor and intoxicated. Of being in the drunk tank and the police hosing them down because one person was shouting, and the impossibility of fighting against the force of water, being pushed across the floor by it.

Then let out, later, into the icy cold, with wet clothes.

From that period, he retained a dislike of the Salvation Army; at their single men's hostel once they'd served him and others donated salmon, and he'd lifted his piece up with his fork and under it the plate teemed with maggots. He was insulted; he gave money away left and right but never gave any to the Salvation Army kettles at Christmas.

When I met him, he had a job and was respected, and he spoke English and French, and never swore, and would not countenance his compatriots speaking badly of women or of others. He said you had to speak up and put a stop to it. You couldn't just sit in silence. He taught me that. And he encouraged me to work hard to learn French in the French classes at CN, which on-train services employees with less seniority, such as myself, could take in the winter instead of being unemployed.

We ate lasagna in a long-gone restaurant on Main Street just north of the Hotel Ivanhoe. The little man would get drunk and flip coins with others, "his friends," for twenty-dollar bills. He bought lottery tickets too, alone and in pools run from under the counter at the Ivanhoe bar.

Sometimes his paycheque lasted one day.

There was only one time, back when the paycheques were issued at the crew office and I was on the road, that he somehow picked up my paycheque for me, and cashed it, and both my cheque and his were all gone when I came back the next day. I told the office never to give him my cheque again.

He gave me money from his next few cheques to pay me back. My paycheque had been invested in some kind of gambling scheme he never expected to lose.

He always had loans from Household Finance and other now vanished "finance companies" that charged usurious rates. I tried to talk him out of them, and into saving first then spending later.

He could be violent when drunk, and there were times when he frightened me and hurt me. Then he was apologetic and handsome again. I thought I could love him as I had loved my Dad who also had been of a temper (though not from drinking). I thought I could avoid the bad times and stay out of trouble.

The sun is rising on the snow as I write this: bright red, a line of light that outlines the stones of the church opposite in Montréal where I live.

The little man has been here in the past, to visit me.

Last night on December 27, 2015, my home phone rang, the

phone with the old number and no answering machine, and it was his cousin Betty from Vancouver calling as she had wanted to tell me he died on December 4, 2015 in St. Paul's Hospital in Vancouver.

He was alone when he died.

They had admitted him earlier and diagnosed pneumonia after he had gone to emergency with difficulty breathing. A couple of hours later, they did a bed check and he was flat-lined. They started his heart again and put him on a respirator but he was brain dead.

In the next morning, they found his cousin who was his next of kin and she asked them to turn off the respirator. He had shown no brain activity; he was dead.

The little man was dead.

He was just seventy-two.

Did you know he had been using a walker the past couple of years, said Betty. No, I said. I knew he had trouble with his heart and was on medication. He died of a heart attack, she said. He had COPD for years too. Well, he smoked so heavily, I said.

Betty told me she knew she had to tell me.

She said she is just winding up the estate, and he'd had a RRIF still from his CN / VIA pension, worth about $12,000. Sylvie, his niece would get it. He would like that, I said. No, he wouldn't, she replied. He got mad at Sylvie in 2010 when Mon Oncle died and Sylvie got the estate as her mother was already dead, and Paul never talked to Sylvie again. Oh, but he could be stubborn, I said. His Dad was always sending him money, she said, he got his share. I am sure of that, I said.

After he left VIA Rail before they could fire him due to his impossible behaviour at work when he was drinking alcohol, he got a job at an old age home, in Burnaby or Surrey. He had to take the bus a long way. He worked in the kitchen, and in the dining room to help the residents eat their meals, and cleaned the dining room afterward. He was impossibly kind to old people always, and kind to his fellow workers. He kept his drinking to a level that enabled him to keep his job.

Later the care home was privatized under some provincial cut-backs and it was bought by an immigrant family who bought several such smaller care homes. The wages of the workers were cut. Many left or were terminated but Paul stayed.

He worked at that work till he retired.

All his life he did work and pay his taxes, despite his alcoholism.

He went out for a few months with a nurse a few years after we split up, but I know that to him he was still married to me forever.

I wanted him to be happy.

Betty said his bank account was overdrawn, and she hadn't talked to him since the summer as his phone had been cut off for nonpayment. She had tried to invite him to their house in Tsawwassen in August for a BBQ, but he felt he shouldn't come as his room was badly infested with bedbugs and he was afraid of bringing bedbug eggs.

Betty was worried about her grandchildren so didn't pursue the invitation further.

When she went to the rooming house hotel on Cordova Street to clean out his things, she found out this was true, and that in fact he had been served with an eviction notice as he had refused to let the management go in to fumigate.

This seemed like stubborn behaviour perhaps but I remember him as someone who would not kill any being, even an insect. Mosquitoes did not bite him, and probably the bedbugs did not bite him either very much or he did not mind it. He had lived with bedbugs before.

There was a restaurant in Chinatown where we always went to eat together and they knew him there and he ordered heaps of food and we brought it home and ate it for days.

He gave money to everyone. He sat with people who were suffering and just tried to be there.

We went together to Postie's funeral. It was in a narrow and starkly lonely room in a funeral home and there were about eight people there. I can't remember if Postie had relatives. His working life had ended before I met him, but yes he had been a letter carrier for the federal post corporation.

Beef with broccoli, shrimp and mixed vegetables, breaded chicken in sweet and sour sauce.

We drank at the Veterans' Club up on Main Street that we called the Legion even though, strictly speaking, it was not a Legion. I found myself drinking too so that he wouldn't drink everything and get too drunk. This was bad logic. I didn't actually like drinking hard liquor. At the bar in the Hotel Ivanhoe too.

We ate meals there in the little restaurant at the back of the bar, with checked tablecloths.

The little man always brought his shirts, work and casual, to the laundry at Main and 16th and had them washed, pressed, starched. The non-work shirts were brought back on hangers with no creases, and the work shirts were folded so that they had perfect creases of a new shirt when he put them on.

On one forearm, the left (or right?), he had a tattoo of a red heart and a banner around it that said *Maman*.

He was meticulously clean, and washed the dishes always, and cooked for me. He had very strict habits; I think they kept him going.

Betty said every book I had published and every letter and card I had ever sent him were in a bag in his room.

It was all contaminated by bedbug eggs though, and everything had to be destroyed.

I hear his voice and remember how he signed his name. Paul.

He called me every Christmas. This year he did not and I did not get a card from him.

There was another restaurant a bit north of the Hotel Ivanhoe that served Portuguese food every Tuesday night and its back room was full of Portuguese people and us eating pork and clams.

His sister Hélène died of cancer after years of struggle, before 2010.

His brother Jean, who'd had a psychic break as a young man and suffered a motor vehicle accident while trying to escape from the mental health facility in Port Coquitlam — pursued, he'd leaped over a small hedge, only to cascade onto the busy Lougheed Highway — was quadriplegic and brain damaged from being hit and dragged by the car; he also died before 2010, of pneumonia in a care home.

At the time of Jean's accident, about a year before I met the little man, his parents came from Montréal and they believed a Catholic god would heal him so they wouldn't allow him to be unplugged. He was in a coma for months then came to, and was very damaged.

I wrote a poem called "Pulling Thru" about a dream I had of the little man and his brother.

In the Gasthaus on Robson Street west of Burrard, we'd eat big schnitzels and drink Blue Nun wine. One night we left the restaurant and he was very drunk and stopped in the street and looked up at a streetlight and thought it was the sun and said what he used to say to the sun: Shine on me, little star.

I still do that to streetlights in his honour. Shine on me, little star.

We visited Jean every week at Riverview Hospital. He laughed a lot but also pulled his finger (he could move one arm a bit) jaggedly across his neck, to ask Paul to kill him.

He wasn't schizophrenic anymore, just the mental age of ten, they said.

The little man said that on the day before the accident, he'd visited Jean and had an argument with him and had left the mental hospital and said he was never coming back to see him.

He said he knew Jean had tried to run away to come to find him in Montréal to apologize.

He blamed himself for Jean's accident.

We'd go twice a year to see his cousin Betty in Surrey and Betty's parents would be there; her Dad was Paul's uncle and a Savard and worked for BC Hydro on a lineman crew. He had done well for himself. Paul's aunt, who was his mom's sister for they were two brothers who married two sisters, always baked me lemon meringue pie, an entire pie, all to myself, as I so loved her pie.

We watched home movies of that family, with Betty as a child running across a lawn, and sometimes, in the later movies, Paul was on the screen. I was impressed; when we were small we had no home movies. This family had moved up in the world.

The balcony in NDG was wood and the wall was stone and his mother wore a flowered dress.

Later that street was repossessed for the building of the Décarie Expressway. The Savards moved a few blocks away and lived practically overlooking the Expressway, I think. It must have been noisy, but the urban held people in thrall then.

When I knew them, years later, the family lived in sleepy Pincourt on l'Île Perrot, an island of the Hochelaga Archipelago to the west of Montréal, in a 1970s modern suburb close to an ancient church and village. Their parish was Notre Dame de Lorette, the patron of air travel and auspicious journeys, in memory of the angels who translated the Blessed Virgin Mary's house from Palestine to Loreto, Italy in 1291, just before the Crusaders were booted from the Holy Land. That's translation for you; it's hard work and sometimes unwanted.

Everyone in the Savard family worked hard. The quiet comfort of l'Île Perrot was well deserved, though it was not without anxieties. It was Jean and Paul who had the "problems."

The little man would call me every year at Christmas.

Betty said he clearly loved me and the personal things of value to him had been my books and letters. You can't bring very much when you move into a room like that, she said, just what means the most to you.

He had always told me to study hard, and he encouraged me to take the Service Manager course at VIA though he himself, with more experience, had not been accepted. He thought women service managers were important. I was the only woman from the West in that first year of the training, 1980. When I was accepted, my Mom and I delayed a long-awaited trip we'd planned to take together to Cuba.

She forgave me, as I was improving myself. Later that fall we went to Crete instead. I still have photos of my mother with a yellow backpack as for I wouldn't let her bring a suitcase.

It was the little man who encouraged me to take railway French classes and to pay attention in the classroom and actually learn while my rail colleagues were fooling around or falling asleep at their desks.

We often ate at the lunch counter in the IGA at Main and 13th when we went to buy groceries. It was part of Paul's routine and he was friendly with the waitresses in their white, almost medical uniforms. Eventually that lunch counter closed down (it was very outdated) and was torn out, and it upset Paul to see it go. For a long time you could see the echoed swoop of the lunch counter sign high up on the wall.

We most often ate clubhouse sandwiches there; they used real chicken and real mayonnaise.

The little man's favourite hockey player was Serge Savard of the Habs. Of course.

When I met him, he had beautiful long sideburns, immaculately groomed.

He shaved by hand. I remember his face covered by foam. The little man was meticulous about shaving carefully and closely. His beard grew so thickly that if he didn't shave for a day or so, his skin started to hurt him.

Our address I will never forget, a basement suite at 15 West 21st Avenue, Vancouver. The owner lived upstairs, an elderly man who had lived there since the house was built (the land was reclaimed in the 1930s from a dump). His name was Tom and he had been a milkman during his working years. He talked of delivering milk in the Great Depression to the rich houses on the hill in Shaughnessy and stealing children's shoes so he could leave them with the milk at the doors of the poor in the other parts of his route, so the children who did not have shoes could have shoes.

You had to have shoes to go to school.

I remember Tom's house so well. It was after the death of his wife and then his own death that Tom's son sold the house. Paul had to move and went to live downtown in a flophouse hotel. The house you see now on Google Street View on West 21st Avenue is not the same house, but appears to have been built on the base of the old.

The little man had dreams of buying his own furniture one day but never did; he always only lived in furnished tiny places.

The little man was a tremendous cook.

He insisted shepherd's pie was really called Chinese Pie, and that the comma was a virgule, and he called pasta paste. He was a stubborn man.

He admired Pierre Elliot Trudeau.

Québec's St. Charles River in the Wendat language is

Akiawenrahk which means Trout River. I can't imagine the little man fishing for trout in a river.

Once we sat in Grandview Park near Commercial Drive in Vancouver at midnight and a young Indigenous guy started talking to Paul. He was alone and a bit gleeful, glue maybe. He had a bag of oranges from a corner grocery and a large bottle of vodka, and he sat with us and invited us to have a drink with him. After cutting the oranges he'd squeeze some of the juice into his mouth, then fill up the space in the cut orange with vodka and pass it to us to share a drink.

There was a fountain behind us. The brassy noise of that fountain against the dark.

It was not raining but had been earlier. The whole city of Vancouver had a different view and cadence from where we three sat, peaceably talking about life and hopes for the future.

Betty said his niece Sylvie is going through a hard time in her own life. Betty told me she feeds nineteen cats. She ought to stop doing that, she said to me.

That makes sense to me though I can understand by that one detail that she is related to the little man.

I don't know what else to say but I will add to this later until it contains everything I remember about Paul Émile Savard.

His life was worth living and these moments are his legacy.

When I was in Vancouver from January to March of 2015, I thought of him but did not let him know I was in town. I was ashamed of this, really, and still am. Yet I knew that mentally I could not be drawn into the spiral of his life, and I knew that he would be hurt if I didn't.

Maybe I just wanted to remember the old Paul, "the Old G." as I called him in the dedication printed in *Empire, York Street*.

It's 11 a.m. and I haven't done anything yet but feel stricken and write these words.

Did no one ever take his picture?

I once had a black and white photo of him sleeping just outside the train station in Vancouver in Thornton Park, named for Sir Henry, modernizer of the CNR, and built on rich Chilliwack black soil. He was wearing a white shirt with fine blue stripes, rolled up two times at the sleeves, and jeans with a crease ironed into them, and slept with one arm under his head. He was in the shade of a giant catalpa; it was late afternoon and the shadows of near-sunset were long across the grass of the park.

I took the photo as I didn't want to wake him right away; he looked so peaceful. He hadn't come home that afternoon and so I'd gone out to look for him, fearing that he wouldn't come home until the next day.

Today I feel I am out looking for him again. The little man.

I loved him because he seemed neither like a man nor like a woman to me but like an angel. I could tell by his perfect small hands and by his ears, which were straight and tall and had beautiful lobes.

Shine on him, little star. Shine on our Paul.

28 December 2015, Montréal

2

Of the furniture in the basement apartment at Tom's, only the TV was Paul's.

I'm trying to remember what he wore to bed, I think it was a white undershirt only. Then he'd get up on his days at home and don a magnificent old bathrobe. He'd make himself an instant coffee and light a cigarette and sit in the over-uphol-stered chair from the 1940s in the living room area beside the bed.

He'd sit in that one armchair and watch TV in French until the rays of afternoon lit up the small window above.

Sometimes I'd sit in the chair with him. I remember a movie with a man falling and falling and yelling "salaud!" and the little man told me it meant bastard. I was learning French and watching French films was supposed to help me, though really I understood little at that point and they were not my kind of films anyway.

He probably was only dispensed a small part of that RRIF fund every year. I know there is a minimum the bank must dispense every year but is there a maximum? Did he know he could have taken more out? Did the bank never tell him?

He probably owed money to his friends when he died. Though he only borrowed what he needed, he often had to engage in a redistribution of wealth amongst those closest to him. In about 1450, it was called "to robbe Petyr & geve it Poule," and was included in 1546 by John Heywood in his book of "all the prouerbes in the englishe tongue." In his case, though, the little man never really ended up with the money, and no Petyr was robbed.

In French the same expression, "découvrir Saint Pierre pour couvrir Saint Paul," literally means to strip Peter to clothe Paul.

Our Paul would not have stripped Pierre.

To him the spirit was in everything, even the bedbugs. I know he would have believed they were no less than he himself.

Though once I remember he was not sleeping beside me and I got up and went out of the little basement suite as he was not inside anywhere. It was summer, late night, 3 a.m. or so. He was wearing the bathrobe and was out on the lawn with the landlord Tom; with flashlights they were drawing out the cutworms that lived in the lawn and made it lumpy, and, bizarrely, cutting them in half with the hedge clippers. He was helping Tom do this. It shocked me but I just went in and went back to bed.

Of course he was at least half-drunk. Maybe he'd been upstairs that evening playing cards with Tom.

The basement suite was dark and smoke-flavoured and brown-panelled inside and had a fireplace between the TV and bed where we burned those rolled-up prepackaged logs in the winter. I still have a photo in black and white of a fire burning; the photograph is anonymous completely but I know it depicts that house.

Otherwise it is a meaningless photograph.

It's almost 4 a.m. and I have been sleeping but I had a bad dream where I still worked for VIA Rail but had a bunch of credit cards not mine, not stolen, but that I'd improperly used to help someone. I was afraid I'd be found out.

I think I was helping him.

In a sense, I just realized, I actually did get my Christmas phone call from him but it was the voice of his cousin Betty.

It's Betty, she said. I'm phoning about Paul.

Betty who, I said? Paul who? I know two Bettys and three Pauls at least. Is this Erín Moure she said. Yes, I said. It's Paul's cousin Betty, Paul Savard.

My stomach clenched. I knew there was only one reason for her call.

She said I gave his life meaning but that was not for her to say.

What she really meant, or what she could have said, was that she herself finally realized that her cousin's life had been meaningful, because he had loved someone.

Like at the beginning of my book *Pillage Laud*, where I quoted the Italian author Antonio Tabucchi from *The Last Three Days of Fernando Pessoa*, in which the heteronyms come to their poet Fernando Pessoa in the hospital to bid him farewell. The quote comes from the moment when Álvaro de Campos went to see Pessoa, and Pessoa said to him, go with the gods, as you have loved someone, you are forgiven.

Álvaro de Campos was the heteronym who was probably gay. In *Pillage Laud*, the epigraph is in French, but I will translate it here into English. It is a conversation.

> "Did you truly love some one?" murmured Pessoa.
> "I truly loved someone," answered Campos in a low voice.
> "Alright, I absolve you," said Pessoa, "I absolve you; here I thought that in your life all that you had ever loved was theory."
> "No," said Campos, coming closer to the bed, "I also loved life, and if in my furious and futurist odes I poked fun, if in my nihilist poetry I destroyed everything even myself, know that I loved in my life, with conscious pain."

Pessoa raised his hand in an esoteric gesture. He said: "I absolve you, Álvaro, go with the eternal gods, if you had a single love, you are absolved, because you are a human person, it is your humanity that absolves you."

"Do you mind if I smoke?" Campos asked.

That book was made into a play and Denis Marleau directed it in Montréal, Théâtre Ubu, and I think it was Marleau's first use of a robot and hologram faces, as one heteronym was played by a robot.

I think that when Betty cleaned out his room into bags and then opened them not inside her house because of the bed-bugs but at the end of her garden, and found my letters to Paul and all my books of poetry, she realized herself that Paul had loved someone.

And to me, as to Pessoa, because he loved someone, he is absolved; his humanity absolves him.

I went to see that play in 1997 with Robert Majzels and Claire Huot, but Claire had to leave in the middle as as she realized she'd left a roast at home in the oven, and the oven on. The roast was burnt up, she told us later, but there was no fire.

I remember so many times at night walking toward home with Paul on West 21st Avenue from Main Street under the huge trees.

Sometimes we walked the other way along West 21st, to Cambie Street, and went into the White Spot at the corner of West 12th Avenue, where we'd drink coffee and eat a hamburger with some kind of special sauce.

Those hamburgers still exist but they don't taste anywhere near the same. You could order lots of sauce by asking for your hamburger "Triple O," or OOO, which was the waitresses' code for lots of sauce. The hamburger would arrive, well, dripping.

The bun had a kind of texture that no other bun had on any other hamburger. The burger always arrived on a small plate topped with a slice of dill pickle.

Now I think the restaurants are called Triple O, practically. The one on West 12th is gone.

Art Phillips was mayor of Vancouver. I remember the Burrard Bridge as well. And Paul really just ate those hamburgers because I liked them.

After meeting Paul, I still kept a room in Kitsilano where I wrote poetry when Paul was "on the road." We were two days apart usually in our travel schedules at CN and then VIA as every second day the crew was from Winnipeg not Vancouver.

Wikipedia says: "on January 12, 1977, CN spun off its passenger services as a separate Crown corporation, VIA Rail Canada." We employees were spun off too; suddenly we worked for VIA Rail. We were proud of passenger rail. "In this great land there was a time when the railroad did not run," as the song says, but then it did and that was a deciding factor.

The little man retained something of the time-before, though you could not possibly imagine him in the woods, or fishing trout.

On our work schedules, normally he left two days before me and I read and wrote for two days. Or I got back to Vancouver and had two days to write before he came home.

He never or rarely came to the room in Kitsilano. I had a mattress there and a little kitchen where I cooked on a sort of stove like the one the painter Anthony Burnham has in his studio in Montréal, and the bathroom was in the hall. There were thirteen rooms and three shared bathrooms there.

Years later when the building, a large "conversion house," was slated to be altered and gentrified, I moved into a small place closer to our basement suite, beside Fire Hall No. 3 at Quebec Street and 12th Avenue. The little man was upset because this apartment had two rooms and one was a real kitchen.

He thought I was moving out and maybe I was.

He was upset when I took my clothes from the closet of the basement suite at Tom's and moved them all to the little apartment on Quebec. I remember the day I did this. What did it mean? I didn't know and didn't dare to ask myself; I just wanted to move my clothes.

I also smoked cigarettes; I'd quit smoking when I first met Paul, but started again because he smoked and so I smoked too. I knew it was stupid to smoke but I figured it was inevitable. The doctor told me to quit and said my asthma meant every cigarette I smoked was like a normal person smoking three.

I did quit again in the apartment on Quebec Street as I started to get out of breath climbing even one floor of stairs. The cost of a package of Player's Mild, which I smoked then, cost $1.01 when I quit. I bought them in a corner store at Main and 12th that is no longer there.

I always went home to the basement suite to eat dinner with Paul.

Normally if I wake up and think of things to write at this hour (it's 4:30 a.m.) I don't write them down the way I did when I was younger, let alone get up like this and start typing.

I too at night look up to the streetlights in the rain or snow and say Shine on me, little star.

Later I asked him who he thought he was talking to and he said the sun.

But the streetlight is not the sun, I said. He looked at me as if I were absurd.

The sun in the spring would make him sneeze. We would

26

stand at the bus stop at Main Street and 20th Avenue to head down to the Hotel Ivanhoe and he would be sneezing like mad into his sleeve, the sun dappling him.

He made really good spaghetti sauce. It had to be cooked all day. That and *pâté chinois*, the chinese pie, or chopped pie. We ate it always with ketchup.

It's the only thing I like ketchup on, to tell the truth. The last ray of sunset would stream down into the basement suite from the little high window above the kitchen table, lighting up the smoke-stained lacquer of the walls and cupboards, and we'd eat shepherd's pie, oops, *pâté chinois*. The sunset: it had to be summer. The back door would have been open too.

Before there was ever anything like a food processor, there was the Chinese hat or *chinois*. It was a conical sieve, with a metal support system and a wider mesh than a regular sieve. You could use a pestle to push cooked food through it to make a kind of rough puree. You could also strain out big lumps and if you laid a cheesecloth in it, you could strain out all lumps.

I always figured the *pâté chinois* was not really Chinese but was ground-up pie or chopped pie, related to the hat.

Paul and I had both worked as cooks. I worked as a second cook in the dining car under the chef, or as a dining-car waitress when there were no cook positions that my seniority allowed me to "hold." Paul, when I met him, had recently returned from "college," which is to say rehabilitation for alcoholism. My colleagues were very happy to see him back. He was not a joker; he was serious about his work.

The little man had previously been a private-car steward, a prestigious job that involved maintaining a private car for an executive of CN. He was a butler, footman, cook, and housekeeper all in one and wore a better livery than we did. We passed these private cars at times on the station siding at Edmonton, and Paul always got down from our train, the SuperContinental, and went over to shoot the breeze with the private-car stewards on duty.

The railway was pretty run-down at the time I started to work for CN, and it was the end of the era of nice uniforms. With the onset of VIA, stewards still did wear grey blazers and black trousers; sleeping car conductors wore dark grey suits with white shirts and black four-in-hand ties. Waiters once wore snappy short red cotton jackets with black trousers, white shirts and ties, and long aprons. After a certain point, though, it was cheap red polyester jackets with mandarin collars for the men, no shirts or ties, and the long apron. Older waiters despised this look and wore the neck open, with white shirts and black ties regardless. Women wait staff wore a blue-and-red striped short apron and navy blue slacks.

There were no strings on the long apron; you had to attach your own to the apron cloth, using small metal and plastic garter clips, like the ones for stockings.

The photos of the little man beside his private car in his livery were impressive and he was respected by everyone, despite his disability with alcohol.

The little man also loved porterhouse steaks. They were the most expensive cut of meat, with the loin on one side of the bone and the tenderloin on the other. He cooked them rare in a frypan on top of the stove, or sometimes outside on the little hibachi in summer. And he made mashed potatoes with a bit of chopped onion and milk and a large gob of butter. I don't use the butter myself but otherwise since I've known him, I've always put finely chopped onion in mashed potatoes when I make them. So finely chopped no one really knows they are there.

Once, Paul decided on a regime in which he would only drink one drink a day. The rationing system was intended to keep him employed and to keep him from losing me. But as the days went by, he kept buying bigger and bigger glasses so as to fit more whisky into them. He drank Canadian Club rye then, with ginger ale.

I remember him in the end pouring a whole mickey of rye into a very tall glass, then adding a drop of ginger ale. As he sipped it down, he'd add more ginger ale. He was very patient and it took him nearly all day to drink it.

When it was finished, he would drink a few beers. Beer was not really alcohol unless you drank more than six.

I didn't really think this plan was going to work but it was not my watch to say so. Around the same time, the dog I grew up with in Calgary went blind; my mother told me in a letter as she did not like to call long-distance, which was expensive then. I wrote the poem called "Tricks," in which the giant glass of whisky appears.

I always did like opening the fridge and finding square waxed boxes of Chinese food take-out from our wandering adventures of the day before. I could still eat Chinese food in those days (saté sauce was not omnipresent in Chinese restaurants, so I could avoid peanut). We had no microwave oven so we would heat up this delicious food in a cast-iron pan on the stove.

The little man did not eat peanut butter so I was safe with him.

Once, he made me go to Woodward's Photo Studio in the Woodward's department store on Hastings Street in the Downtown Eastside and have a portrait taken of myself as a present for my mother. He wanted a copy too. I bought two frames of wood as well, that could be leaned on a mantle.

The little man and my mother both had the same framed picture of me on their mantles.

I always disliked that photograph but Paul thought I was beautiful in it.

When my mother died in 2007, I finally was able to throw out her copy of the photo. I don't know if Paul still had his but I guess if he did it went with the bedbugs into the fire.

I can't remember what we ate for breakfast in those days. I think I ate leftover Chinese food a lot, for breakfast and for lunch. The little man always cooked dinner.

He had a strange method for reheating any leftover shepherd's pie. Part of the idea of making *pâté chinois* is to have leftovers, of course. I remember it bubbling in the pan, burning slightly crisp at the bottom, with fat from the meat leaking out in tiny bubbles up over the potatoes.

I'd better go back to bed now.

Paul could really have used the money in that RRIF. He would have paid off everything he owed, and maybe moved to a hotel less problematic. Though he was already on West Cordova, technically in Gastown not the Downtown Eastside. Maybe he didn't know that you could change the amount you got from an RRIF, and get any amount. Or maybe he was trying to play it out as a pension, but I don't think so.

With $12,000 in the RRIF and the minimum withdrawal being 5% he would have got $600 per year in pension from his years at CN and VIA Rail.

I'm wrong. I just learned there *is* a maximum because it's not a RRIF he would have had but a LRIF as the funds came not from him but from his past employer. On the Internet it says:

"If your LIF or LRIF is federally regulated, the percentages in the table from the website of the Office of the Superintendent of Financial Institutions (OSFI) can be used to determine the maximum annual withdrawal for the year. The percentages in the table change each year, as they are determined by reference to the CANSIM B14013 rate in effect during the previous month of November."

At www.osfi-bsif.gc.ca/Eng/pp-rr/faq/Pages/lif-frv.aspx it says that for 2016 the maximum amount would have been 6.659% or $799.08 for the year. VIA Rail is federally regulated.

The maximum amount of CPP would have been $12,780 for 2015 and the maximum OAS (2014) would have been $6,676.59 for the year. I don't know if the little man got the max, as his income during his last twenty working years was quite low, from the old folks' home. If I add those numbers together, though, the maximum he could have earned would be $20,255.67. The poverty line in 2014 for one person in Vancouver was $23,647.

I think with his income during his working years, the little man would have had less CPP than in my calculation. I myself, who worked as long as Paul did but made somewhat more money, will only have a maximum CPP of $10,200 per year when I am 65. So maybe I will use my figure, and then the total of the three numbers adds up to a pension of $17,675.67 for the year for the little man.

The rent on a room at the Hildon Hotel, according to Kijiji

this week, is $525 or $6,300 per year. Paul would have been left with $11,375.67 after rent, or $947.97 each month. That was about $31.59 per day for eating restaurant meals and buying his sundries and beer. For doing his laundry and buying clothes and buying shaving foam and razors and soap and shampoo. You could eat budget meals in Vancouver for about $22, maybe, leaving just under $10 for Paul to buy his beers. A cheap beer probably costs $3.

He must have eaten some meals at a soup kitchen or mission so as to be able to drink enough not to feel ravaged by the lack of it and his cells all screaming at him.

I think his account was overdrawn because it was the beginning of the month when he died, and he hadn't received his pensions yet. Betty did say that the December pensions gave her enough money to have Paul cremated. Maybe the monthly total of the pensions was around $800, then. I think that poor people can be cremated for around $800.

3

I won't get a Christmas card from him this year. I will never get a Christmas card from him again.

He always bought special cards for me, overflowing with the sentiments of friends forever. The last one he sent, I think he was in pain when he wrote it, he just signed it *Paul*.

I had never had a card from him before with just his name. He always signed the word *Paul* on an uphill line, with a scribbled flourish under the letters, and on the left side of the card, wrote me a note.

His signature was elegant.

I can still imitate it.

At bedbugregistry.com on the Internet you can read reports of the bedbugs in the rooming house hotel where the little man lived. On September 20, 2015, a man on disability allowance who lived there wrote:

"I awoke again this morning with a bedbug biting me. Always around 4 o'clock in the morning. I don't have many, just one or two that seem to find me in my steel framed futon. They must be falling from the other side of the future ceiling here."

The last sentence doesn't seem to make sense at first, the bedbugs falling from the other side of the future ceiling. But it does make sense, because a floor becomes a ceiling in the future, if there is falling.

It's December 30, after 9 a.m. and I am up with a cup of coffee. I lay in bed awhile beside the beautiful B., listening to the road graders outside on the street clearing the snow into windrows for the snowthrowers and trucks, and I realized that it's the second last day of the year.

I've slept in, but nothing pressed me to get up. I think about the little man waking up in his rented room. He liked to sleep later than me, like B.

In the Kijiji ad on the Internet, I found a photograph of a room for rent at 50 West Cordova, in the Hildon Hotel, above the bar called The Bourbon, where the little man lived for years. The room has a window full of light, stark even, and a single bed with no sheets on it but yes a white mattress cover, and the room also holds a small fridge, and an un-upholstered chair.

I guess that in a residential hotel, you have to bring your own sheets.

And the bathroom is down the hall.

The little man first lived in another residential hotel or flop-house in Gastown. My 1996 address book shows it as being at 404 Abbott Street, Room 206. A building known as Abbott Mansion, completed in 1909 by Vancouver entrepreneur Loo Gee Wing. Wing also built the building that held Ho Ho Chop Suey on West Pender, where Paul and I would eat in Chinatown. Life is full of coincidences; they are clues to viewing what I think of as the hidden structure of the world.

The little man once told me you had to put boots on to go to the bathroom down the hall at the Abbott Mansion as there were so many used needles in the hallway and in the bathroom and it was important not to step on them. In that place the owners only cleaned the bathroom once a week so that was when Paul took a shower.

In our life he took a shower every day. He ironed a crease into his jeans and his shirts were always crisp. His casual look was to roll his sleeves just twice, equally, so you could see just a bit of the tattoo on his forearm. The hair on his arm was long, straight, as neat as he always was.

In 1999 and 2000 and 2001, he was still in the Abbott Mansion but in room 307. On the Internet it says that the building was renovated in 1999 and in a 2015 statement, Central City, its operator, claimed that it was a safe place to live. "Thanks to Central City Foundation donors, the Abbott provides clean, safe and reliable housing for those with low incomes, with rents at or below the shelter allowance provided by social assistance. Management strives to keep the building free of the drug dealing, violence and harassment common in Downtown Eastside hotels, providing a safe haven for its tenants while serving as an example for other buildings in the neighbourhood."

Yet by 2003 (I have no address book for 2002), Paul had moved to the Hildon Hotel, two streets away from the Mansion. I recall he said it had been renovated a while before, and he said it was cleaner and the bathroom in the hall was cleaned every day. The price per month was higher than the welfare supplement for housing. Thus there were fewer folk with serious substance abuse difficulties and the dealers that they attract, as it took at least a disability allowance to afford the Hildon. In 2003, I had no phone number for Paul Savard so he must have got a phone later, or he hadn't yet given me his number.

I never did imagine the bedbugs there, I always imagined it as renovated, until Betty told me on the day after Boxing Day of 2015 about the "severe infestation" in Paul's room.

Whatever would have happened to him had he been evicted? Where would he have gone? He was ill and fragile.

On bedbugregistry.com in the entry for the Hildon there is another despairing commentary, from November of 2015, about the elevator being broken for weeks, in the month before the little man died. I try to imagine Paul, with his walker and difficulty breathing, climbing a staircase to his fifth-floor room.

There is no website for brokenelevatorinroominghouse-registry.com.

I just read on the Internet that they call those places in the Downtown Eastside SRO hotels: single room occupancy hotels. The name doesn't make any sense to me. Do people occupy more than one room in classier hotels?

Other commentary on the bedbug website indicates the residents felt the management at 50 West Cordova were mean and intrusive. The owners of the hotel apparently also owned the adjoining Army & Navy department store; the hotel managers were employees. Paul had originally said he had a good relationship with the management; so I don't know why, years later, he wouldn't let them into his room.

Cordova Street was named after a late-eighteenth-century Spanish military commander and Viceroy of Mexico, His Excellency Bailio Frey Don Antonio Maria Bucareli y Ursúa Henestrosa Lasso de la Vega Villacis y Córdoba.

I imagine Paul waking up and remaining in bed and watching the light outside and trying to imagine from the sounds what was happening on the street below. Or maybe his room looked over the alley instead. The light of day is moderated by the overcast cloud of Vancouver and Paul lighting up a cigarette.

He smoked Craven A's. No one else I knew smoked Craven A's.

I put Craven A's into a poem many years ago and one day will publish that poem. It was accepted by an American magazine but never appeared and later the poetry editor, Ben Lerner, wrote me to apologize and say he thought the magazine had gone under. That was okay with me; I was just happy Ben Lerner had liked the poem.

Rothmans Benson & Hedges own Craven A and Philip Morris International owns RBH. Wikipedia says Craven A is part of a "premium brand strategy" in Canada, and that the brand has experienced "long-term declines in market share" since the elimination of sponsorship activities in 2003, in accordance with the federal health law restricting promotion of tobacco. The brand's last sponsorship was of the Just for Laughs Comedy Tour.

A look at the Philip Morris parent website shows that the manufacturer of cigarettes no longer finds them innocuous. It says: "More than 5,000 chemicals — or smoke constituents — are formed when tobacco is burned. More than 100 of these smoke constituents have been identified by public health authorities as causes or potential causes of smoking related diseases, including cardiovascular disease (heart disease), lung cancer, and chronic obstructive pulmonary disease (emphysema, chronic bronchitis). Smokers are far more likely to become sick with one of these diseases than non-smokers. In addition, smoking is addictive, and it can be very difficult to stop smoking. These are the views of leading scientific and public health organizations around the world. They are also the views of Philip Morris International."

The little man always smoked two packs of cigarettes a day made by that company. He coughed a lot even when I knew him.

I met him when he was thirty-three and so I must have been twenty-one. I only realize now that he was the first person I ever fell in love with, in the way that one falls in love then gets together with the person and tries to make a life together.

Smoking killed him, not drinking, and not sadness, and not being alone. He was relatively good at being alone.

Each part of life even the sun on the wall was meaningful to the little man. And he cared about others.

He was a little Levinasian man, and a little Rancièrian man, though he would not have put it that way, having never read Levinas or Rancière.

After breakfast on the day after I found out from his cousin Betty that he had died, I googled his last address. The first thing on the list was the bedbug report.* On April 4, 2009,

---

* *"Name Redacted, on 09/20/2015*: Hello: This is actually called the Hildon Hotel (with a 'D'), the bar below is called the Bourbon. Employees from either establishment have access to both Offices here. Two separate business entities with one set of Staff & Management. Robbie Verse extends himself to the Public as a Bourbon Pub Representative. To the Tenants here he is merely the executive Branch of the Residential Management. He signs our eviction notices and enters our rooms to verbally and physically harass us. If the Robbie below is the same Robbie here . . . that Robbie is a fraudulent and a physio-logically disturbed man. I awoke again this morning with a bedbug biting

one person had written: "I live in the Bourbon Hotel, many of my neighbors and myself are being eatin alive by bedbugs every night."

From Wikipedia: "While VIA is an independent federal Crown corporation mandated to operate as a business, it is hindered by the fact that it was created by an Order in Council of the Privy Council and not from legislation passed by Parliament. If VIA were enabled by legislation, the company could seek funding on open money markets as Crown corporations such as CN have done in the past. It is largely for this reason that critics say VIA is vulnerable to federal budget cuts and continues to answer first to its political masters, as opposed to the business decisions needed to ensure the viability of intercity passenger rail service."

In the basement apartment, when the little man would watch TV, I would read books. Sometimes I would read him poetry out loud.

I was probably the only one who had ever done this for him.

---

me. Always around 4 o'clock in the morning. I don't have many, just one or two that seem to find me in my steel framed futon. They must be falling from the other side of the future ceiling here. You see, Robbie is selective about which rooms he cleans before renting. Mine was not cleaned at all, nor was it painted. There must be years and years of filth stored in the space between the future ceiling and the ceiling proper that is now falling on me constantly as I sit in this room. Disgusting . . . huge Godzilla sized disgusting. The Building is owned by the same people who own the Arty & Wavy Dept. Store chain. Both Robbie and Ms. Vicar of the Dept. Store drive about town here in their luxury vehicles, while we are treated more like cargo than like people . . . people who's money is being spent by Robbie."

There's something else I am forgetting to say and it makes me restless at night.

I don't want the little man to disappear and this is the third day I am writing down everything I know about him.

I am sitting shiva for the little man, even though he died December 4. I only found out December 27 in the evening so I started then. 28, 29, 30.

Shiva means "seven" and refers to Genesis, and Joseph's mourning of his father Jacob for seven days.

I have torn my coat. To sit shiva you have to tear your coat or wear a torn piece of cloth, an outer garment. I think it is appropriate to tear my coat.

Leaving the shiva house is permitted in cases when human life is in danger or when something must be done to prevent another from suffering and no one else can go. I am not really sitting shiva properly as I do leave the house.

The little man visited me here in Montréal a few times over the years, and so I think this can be a shiva house. In it, I think of the room where the little man lived in Vancouver.

It is very quiet except for the sound of the TV.

I don't have a TV, though B. and I are thinking of buying a screen to watch movies at home on something bigger than the iPad.

At Aish.com, you can find the traditional words of comfort to one who mourns. It says that there is no consolation, which is true, and it says: "Consolation is not a natural process." This is also true. It continues: "Neither the passage of time, nor the awkward, well-meaning gestures of others can remove the memory or wipe away the pain. That is why we ask God to comfort the mourner — because we cannot."

The name of God in this case is a name of omnipresence-without-a-name. It is this name that is offered. The *namloz* or nameless, the aspect of God that Judaism recognizes as G*x*d and that reflects our own namelessness on earth. If *xx*d cannot have a name, apart from HaShem, "the name," how can we?

This belief in which omniscience does not have a speakable name is very close to the spirituality of the little man.

Aish.com says further: "In the spiritual reality, nothing is lost: Not the beloved one's purpose, nor their goodness, and nor even their real existence. The soul continues to exist eternally. At the end of life, every soul returns to its *makom*, to its unique 'place' in the 'world.' We tell the mourner: If you could see the *makom* where the deceased now dwells, you'd be comforted."

I am trying to see the *makom* and make it in words for the little man, so his spirit has another place and so that his purpose and goodness are not lost. And so that his life is not, to use a Judith Butler term, ungrievable.

And really it is his purpose and goodness that I am not wanting the world to lose. His name means little: Paul Émile Savard, unless you're me and then it means a lot. To me, every letter of his name is crucial, but to you it could be any name at all.

It is true that his violence under the influence of alcoholic spirits frightened and hurt me but that was not who he was. The spirits of alcohol put the spirit of the good Paul to rest, and let the hurt of the world that had condensed in him appear.

In his *makom*, that hurt is surely gone.

4

I remember us eating big bowls of clam chowder (red or white) at The Only Sea Foods on East Hastings.

The Internet says: "When The Only opened in 1916 at 20 East Hastings, it was a big deal in the busy downtown of that era. Two Greek immigrants, Nick Thodos and Antonio Demetry opened it, in the days when restaurant washrooms were not mandatory. The Only didn't have public washrooms to its dying day, which was in June 2009 (shut down by the city because of vermin, and crack storage). But back in its day, it was the only seafood restaurant in Vancouver (thus the name) and served fish as fresh as can be (never more than a day old) and cooked in the style that the Greek brothers knew, with lemon and butter. The Only had a fabulous neon sign with a sea horse which is in storage with the Downtown Eastside's Portland Society, in hopes of another The Only stepping up to the plate."

The *Vancouver Sun* says it closed because of allegations of drug dealing by its proprietors. About the sign, it says: "The neon sea horse leaping above whitecapped waves is a superb example of the playful, imaginative signs that used to line the city's streets in neon's golden age in the 1940s and 50s. It's a combination of painted sheet metal and neon tubes. In the daytime, the sea horse is green with blue eyes, 'Only' is in white on an amber background and 'Sea Foods' is in amber atop blue waves. At night, it's an orange neon sea horse with red neon eyes, and green neon 'Only' and 'Sea Foods.' In case you don't get the message that it only served seafood, 'Fish,' 'Oysters' and 'Clams' are advertised across the bottom. Ironically, one thing that wasn't on the menu was sea horse."

The customers sat on round stools at a serpentine zinc counter and there was a lot of yelling and steam. You had to eat fast as others were standing at your back ready to take your place on the stools. There were also two booths. We never sat in a booth.

Occasionally it was quieter and the cooks talked to each other and the patrons and there was less steam.

The little man reminds me of the boy with the fox in the essay by Michel Eyquem de Montaigne, as cited by Giorgio Agamben at the beginning of his *L'usage des corps*: "A simple little lad from Lacedaemon, who having stolen a fox cub and hidden it under his tunic (for they feared more the shame of bungled theft than its punishment), endured in silence while the fox gnawed his vitals, rather than letting it be discovered."*

Agamben has, as his second epigraph, fox-words attributed to
Vittorio Sereni, "[La vie,] c'est ce renard dérobé que le garçon
cachait sous ses vêtements et qui lui rongeait le flanc." "[Life]
is the nabbed fox the boy hid in his cloak though it gnawed
open his side." It's from a Sereni poem called "Appuntamento
a ora insolita" or "Meeting at a Strange Hour." And now I've
read the Sereni poem on Google Books in Italian and in
English, I see it's not life that is the fox at all; that's Agamben
side-stepping: the fox of Sereni is joy. Sereni's work is collected
in English in *The Selected Poetry and Prose of Vittorio Sereni:
A Bilingual Edition*, translated by Marcus Perryman and Peter
Robinson. The e-book is $4.18 and is really worth it.

The fox is borne like a wound through the dazzling streets, the
poem says. The poet's voice in the poem talks directly to joy,
"my joy, beside me once more after a short estrangement." By
the end of the poem, joy is gone.

I won't get to see the socialist city either, I think. That's also a
line in the poem.

---

* Translated by the author. The real Montaigne quote is: « un enfant de
Lacedemone se laissa deschirer tout le ventre à un renardeau, qu'il avoit
desrobé, et le tenoit caché soubs sa robe, jusques à mourir plustost que de
descouvrir son larrecin. » The boy dies from his own persistence at concealing
an animal. But I see it as an act of symbiosis and protective love. Plus Montaigne's spelling fills me with awareness that his very accent is embedded in the
markings of his prose, which amazes me (I hope you can hear my accent as you
read, from Calgary Alberta, 1955).

As the little man walked down the streets of downtown Vancouver, back when we were together, the fox that he was protecting in his coat ate out of his side.

I tear my coat.

5

Making "christmas-cake spiced roast vegetable soup" for B.
She's still fragile from the infection she contracted in Calgary
in mid-month and needs liquid nutrition until she can eat
solids again.

I am researching the Chinese restaurants along East Pender
in Vancouver in the 1970s to try to find the one that the little
man and I liked best. We did go to the Ho Inn on the north
side of the street but often the owner would get angry upon
seeing Paul and kick us out. He'd had enough of Paul's ornery
stubborn obstreperous behaviour, and he knew Paul from his
days on the street so was already suspicious. We'd cross the
street to the Ho Ho.

Paul had spent some kind of time on the street after losing a
job and before working for CN then VIA. He did tell me once
a story of a prostitute he was in love with. But that he punched
her once because she had fleas. It was in the morning around
11 a.m. as we walked past the flophouse hotel where they had

lived on Pender, and he pointed the hotel door out to me and told me. I think mostly it was that they both had probably been drinking. It shocked and saddened me that he could behave like that.

He was a most excellent lover, considerate and collaborative and slow and pleasuring.

And it mattered to him. I remember him going on Antabuse for a while to try to stay away from drinking. One of the side effects was damaged virility. I told him I didn't mind; it was more important to try to stop drinking. But it made him sad and lonely in his body; he couldn't stand it.

I was thinking the restaurant must have been Chungking Chop Suey or Luk Yee Chop Suey. But I actually think now it was Ho Ho Chop Suey with its incredibly bright sign and sparse but elegant (to me) interior, and two floors, the street floor being more Western. Even if I don't remember it as being on a corner.

The little man was also the first one to say to me, "you're a lesbian." After we'd been making love, in the first weeks of our relationship, he got out of bed in the basement apartment and slumped in the upholstered chair and smoked a Craven A and his eyes went far away and I asked what it was.

"We can't stay together," he said finally, in one sad sentence. "You're a lesbian." He was the first man I'd ever heard utter that word. I myself scarcely knew it. I'd thought all women were

50

attracted to women, but we lived with men. That was all there was to it. And to me Paul was a being-man who had the hands of an angel. Or he was an angel. A being on earth whose definition did not exist among the definitions available to us.

When the passenger train would arrive in Vancouver at dawn, sometimes the little man would come down from West 21st to meet me despite the hour, and with the crew from the dining car we would trek over to the Kam Wai on East Pender; it would be closed but if you knocked they'd open and the room was full of people eating congee and we'd eat bowls of very hot congee with fish for breakfast then go home replete.

All those Chinatown wanderings, and the BBQ pork to go, too. In Mandarin, "star" is 星. In Cantonese, too.

There are also places in my Montréal neighbourhood that are marked by his presence. When the little man would visit me here, he'd come downtown from Île Perrot hours earlier than our meeting time, and wander on St. Denis Street near my house. There used to be a swank bar with pool tables on the second floor of the building at the intersection with Rachel, above the cheap clothing store, Le Château. He'd gone there a few times. Whenever I look up there, over Le Château, I always think of him. On Google Street View, in June of 2015, the second floor is empty and a signboard at the corner offers *Lofts à Louer*. The sign contains a spelling mistake, or maybe it's a pun on money or the lack of it: *Nouvelle Coinstruction*. When I zoom in on-screen, some of the windows have curtains, like Ikea ones, as if they are windows now into people's homes.

I think probably Paul became too poor to drink there. He'd go instead to a place at the corner of Marianne, a block away and across the street: Chez Dany, a pizza-by-the-slice joint with a blue awning, where they also sell beer in bottles. And hamburgers, poutine, pogos with fried potatoes. There's an ATM there and Wi-Fi Gratuit. Paul didn't need Wi-Fi. He'd have a couple of beers there before coming to my house. I try to look inside on Street View but all I can see are reflections of the windows of the fancier restaurant across the street.

Funnily I only remember two things about his various visits. That once we went in a taxi to Place Jacques Cartier in Vieux Montréal, and we sat inside Le Fripon ("Homard, Moules, Sans oublier nos succulentes pièces de viande") at a window and ate lobster. Paul checked to make sure the lobster were alive to start with, as in those days prepared seafood was pretty contaminated with sulphites, which would give me anaphylactic reactions, just as peanuts would.

He went with the waiter to look at the lobsters in their tank of water in the kitchen. Le Fripon has existed since 1972. It would not have been there when Paul lived in Montréal, but it seemed to suit him somehow, I mean, its décor. From another era, not yet bohemian, when the Quiet Revolution had not yet had its impact on the world.

Another time, I remember, after eating dinner and walking me back to my apartment, he wanted to sleep in the spare room and not go back to Île Perrot. It was late; transit would have been lousy to Pincourt, forty-five kilometres distant. I made him go. Maybe that was mean of me, but I didn't want to wake up to him in my spaces. I think now it was mean of me. But if I could go back, I would probably be mean again. I would feel bad about it but I didn't want him to stay, even in the room next to mine.

I don't think this makes me a bad person, but maybe it does. It is a memory, though, and I have to admit it, even if it now humiliates me.

In the Hotel Ivanhoe bar in Vancouver by the VIA train station, Paul had played pool and was good at it; I admired him and liked to watch. Sometimes he'd get me to play against him, and would advise me on shots, or even take my shots for me, then go to the bar and get the key to get the ball back, place it again, and let me try. They liked him at the bar; they always gave him the key. They knew he was not cheating them, but teaching. He played regularly but always used one of the house cues; he wasn't a snob about carrying around his own special cue in a leather case.

If there were arguments between patrons that broke into fights, he'd always jump up to settle people down. He was smaller than most men, but he'd jump up anyhow and put his body between the fighters and his arms out to stop their arms from delivering blows. The little man had a kind of fairness about him. People knew and did settle down, and Paul would come back and sit down with me again, a king. A gentle ruffian king.

Judith Butler wrote in her book on performativity and assembly that "though we may legitimately feel that we are vulnerable in some instances and not in others, the condition of our vulnerability is itself not changeable." She writes: "To say that any of us are vulnerable beings is to mark our radical dependency not only on others but on a sustaining and sustainable world." She says that this matters for understanding "who we are as beings who seek to persist, and whose persistence can be imperilled or sustained depending on whether social, economic, and political structures offer sufficient support for a liveable life."

Butler also says that maybe we can rethink Hannah Arendt's view of politics and action so that the body and what bodies require are part of the political. If we are to move forward in any way, we have to rethink what action is. And what it means to politics. Curiously, Agamben (with whom Butler disagrees on some notions) also speaks of the need to rethink the link between politics and action that has been fundamental since Aristotle. He too raises Arendt's name and her notion of the public sphere as being linked to action.

Agamben says action is a term that comes from the judicial-religious sphere. Instead of the idea of action, he tries to think of *usage* as a fundamental political category. The use of the body.

Paul stood up between those who had come to blows, though

the condition of his vulnerability was not changeable. This is a use of the body that is not labour and is not productive, nor is it action. It is a decision of a being for whom persistence is itself a value and life and is incarnated here in our world, at every moment.

To Agamben, the subject (the being with subjectivity) is not outside "action" — does not pre-exist "action" then carry out acts — but is the space of a process that he or she accomplishes as it accomplishes itself through him or her. Action is, rather, like speaking. It is the mean between active and passive verbs. These middle verbs: the agent or subject effects by being affected.

As Agamben summarizes: « le sujet qui accomplit l'action, par le fait même de l'accomplir, n'agit pas transitivement sur un objet mais s'implique et s'affecte d'abord lui-même dans le procès. » The subject who accomplishes the action, by the very fact of accomplishing it, does not act transitively upon an object but is himself implicated and affected by and in the process.

This is what I mean by wanting to say ethics when I say purpose and goodness. The subject (to paraphrase or translate Agamben again) does not dominate the action but is himself the place where action is produced. This is how an ethical subject is constituted, and where our notion of "affect" comes into the picture most fully.

I remember too that Paul was involved every fall and winter

in a massive football pool run out of the Ivanhoe bar; part of it was a draft and you chose your players and invented your own team, and another part focussed all season long on the scores of the games and how far off you were in guessing them. Another VIA service employee seemed to organize and manage the VIA part of the pool. His name was Van. I don't remember his last name but I see in my mind how he looked; he was a family man, a bit portly, but young. His wife was francophone, Acadian from New Brunswick, and a friend of Paul's; her name was Odette. Every week the little man sent in his picks, then watched the games. Behind the bar at the Hotel Ivanhoe, there were charts keeping track of it all, held by the waiters for safekeeping.

There are many ways to constitute the self as the self, but there are also patterns. I am trying to figure out the pattern that is best articulated by the being-man of the little man.

6

In a sense the little man was lucky that his final evening of
difficult breathing took him to St. Paul's Hospital, where he'd
worked in the laundry when he'd first come to Vancouver from
Montréal. That way he didn't die in that bug-infested room
in the hotel. No one would have found him then for days. He
wouldn't have liked the management coming in to find out
why there was a stench coming from under his door.

He would have wanted to be just naturally dead then cremated
and not to be found in that room.

He'd spent so much time beside his brother Jean in the hospital; he wouldn't have minded the hospital. It would have been
a clean place to breathe his last breath.

Of course I am disturbed that he died alone. But then I think
of my Mom dying and me beside her in Calgary all the last
night of her life and almost all the next day; she was aware
of my being there for sure but her molecules were all slowly

saying farewell to this life and that was what she was doing.

I think of Paul's molecules saying their farewell in the hospital in Vancouver with dignity and though it bothers me that he was alone, it was not a bad way to be alone in a task that we each carry out singly, in the end.

Paul lived in the world of dreams as well as in the real world, and his molecules would have been doing the same thing, just letting go slowly. The COPD from his smoking meant that his heart was too weak.

He was possibly malnourished as well, as he had no way to cook. I still don't understand how, being such a great cook, he could just move out of Tom's all those years ago and into a room and never cook a meal again.

Yes, he could have been malnourished; it seems from a comment on bedbugregistry.com that the elevator was broken in the weeks before he died, and I don't know that he went in and out much; he needed a walker and had trouble breathing and how to climb and descend five flights of stairs?

At Riverview Hospital there were almond trees on the hill and you could pick almonds from the ground in the fall. In the spring, the blossoms blew off the trees and stuck to our faces.

After visiting his brother Jean at the Hospital, we would take a taxi into Port Coquitlam proper and eat Italian food in a traditional pizza and Italian place with the typical Italian restaurant '70s décor: tourist posters of Italy, and red and white checked tablecloths. We ate lasagna usually, or baby back ribs. I remember one time I was telling the little man some story and swearing as I told it, and he kicked me and I asked why and he said: don't swear.

The funny thing was he didn't swear. I stopped swearing then and there, except maybe when I hit my thumb with a hammer or my computer is balky.

There were places on Commercial Drive in Vancouver where we ate as well. One of them, Nick's Spaghetti House, is still there. We would eat BBQ baby back ribs with spaghetti and drink the house red wine, which was Italian and cheap but good. Sometimes we'd walk there from Chinatown to eat. I found a photo just now on Facebook of Nick's Spaghetti House and it still has the same décor and photos or paintings of mountains in Italy as it did over thirty years ago. There was another photo, posted on Facebook on the day before my birthday this year, of the very same BBQ ribs and spaghetti.

Five months ago, one person who ate there wrote this on Facebook: "it was a Great Dinner i went there with my mom At 4:00pm today we both ordered the spaghetti and Meatballs with Red Wine the bread and butter was Really good as well it was Delicious."

At times the little man made BBQ back ribs on the BBQ at home, outside the back door. We had a little hibachi and he'd light the coals by pouring a long line of lighter fluid on them

and lighting a match. Once he lit his arm on fire. I wrote a
poem where that appeared, and the poem was made into a
broadsheet by Lazara Press run by Penny Goldsmith. Another
time he got mad (drunk) in the middle of cooking and refused
to turn the ribs over. So our dinner got blacker and blacker on
one side until it was crisp all the way through, a kind of ash,
and we had no dinner, our dinner was ruined.

The little man went to bed and I left and went on the bus to
Kitsilano to sleep in my studio.

Once while he was drunk, I admit this, there was a terrifying
event. He pushed me against the kitchen wall and was going to
cut my throat with the carving knife. He had the blade against
my throat. He was smaller than me but much stronger. I was
probably somewhat drunk too.

The eyes of Paul had a completely vacant look. The little
man was not inside them at that moment. There was nobody
inside; there was absolute burnt earth. There was the utter
silence after everything has burned.

I didn't know who or what he was seeing or fighting.

I knew already I would die if he cut me. I thought of what
to do and I just told him quietly that if he hurt me he would
wake up in the morning with a regret so deep and utter that he
would never be able to assuage it for as long as he lived. Paul,
you will not like yourself when you wake up in the morning.
In a calm voice. Not moving but not challenging him either.

He let me free and I ran out the kitchen door and out the back door and up the little steps into the back yard and around the house and along the street till I got to Main Street where I took a bus or a taxi to Kitsilano.

In our latter years, I always kept a five dollar bill folded in four and hidden in my wallet, for a taxi.

But I don't want anyone to remember Paul as the body of the little man turned into a void by alcohol; this was not Paul. This was not the man who called me in Montréal every Christmas and said: *Hey there, Toots, how's it goin'?*

Shine on each of us, little star.

7

He was always impeccably dressed when I saw him. The little man was well-groomed: his hair was cut, and he shaved daily, and even a second time in the evening if we went out, and he wore clean and pressed clothes. Down and out didn't apply to the little man.

He wasn't down, but he was an alcoholic, one who had found a way of living with a ravaging addiction. A proud man, he worked all his life, until the age of sixty-five. His last job, from which he'd retired, was as a helper in a seniors' home in the kitchen and dining room and he spoke fondly of the residents, the families, the staff members there. He paid his taxes, and actually died with $12,000 in a locked-in pension fund from his days at VIA Rail (the days when we were together . . . which ended thirty-three years ago).

I've been reading the reviews on Yelp.ca of Nick's Spaghetti House on Commercial Drive all afternoon. I can't get the place out of my head. Some say it is the last old-style Italian joint in Vancouver and some say the waitresses ignored them and the pasta sauce was runny.

To my mind, they served good and copious home-cooked food.

Thinking of how Paul smoked heavily all his life too, which is really what killed him; he had COPD and heart problems. Funnily enough, alcoholism didn't kill him.

And his account was overdrawn and his phone had been cut off for months for non-payment, and he was about to be evicted for not letting the management in to fumigate. But bugs didn't bite him, and he cared for all living things. Even vermin.

My friend Pam suggested I would feel better if I could talk to his friends. But I am not sure.

I am sure he had friends in the bars where he drank, each day quietly rationing out his beers. But I don't know them. He didn't drink in the bar in the hotel where he lived, as it was a hipster western bar with live music and a mechanical bucking bull.

His sister and brother and parents are all dead; he outlived them. I don't know how to find his one niece in Montréal, but I used *69 to phone Betty back and left my number on her voicemail to give to Sylvie in case she would like to call me when she receives the ashes of the little man in Montréal. I'd be glad to go pay my respects in some way in her company.

It's kind of absurd to think she'd want to call me, though. My heart sinks; I want to hope for this absurdity as long as I can.

I did talk to my brothers, who were sad too; they both remember the little man, of course. My parents would have remembered him but they are dead. My good friend Marianne in Australia would remember him.

I am glad his cousin Betty found my number in his address book when, with the building management, she cleaned out the little man's room. She said she realized that his most valued possessions (which he kept in a garbage bag to try to keep the bedbugs out, but the place was really infested and the bag was destroyed with everything else but the address book and his tax and bank records) were my poetry books and all the letters and cards I had sent him for over thirty years. His cousin said she knew then that she had to phone me, and she tried several times, but she was calling a landline number I rarely use, and there is no voicemail on it, and I was in Calgary, not Montréal, helping B. through her health difficulties, when Paul died. His cousin said to me: you brought meaning to his life.

I still hear his voice on the phone saying *Hey there, Toots! Heh heh heh*.

Still he is someone whose life was largely invisible. You won't find him on the Internet anywhere.

The little man had grown up poor, and thus had only a Grade

7 education, as that was the end of public schooling in French in Québec until the mid-to-late sixties, when education was reorganized and CEGEPs invented and public school was created from Grade 1 to 11 instead of just to Grade 7. The system itself, in his day, preyed on poor French-speaking youth, in fact. It wasn't just English oppression of the French-speaking majority, it was the Catholic Church and their grip on all systems that today we know are better off secular.

If you let someone be educated only for seven years, what can they do but work for others at menial jobs?

Paul used to read the newspaper. He bought it every day. He encouraged me to take French and to be serious about the French courses offered to us by CN and then VIA when we were unemployed in the winter. I did. I learned. Did I learn? I learned.

He was well-groomed, the little man, but when he was drunk, no one could understand him. Eventually, I had to stop telling him about my poetry readings, as he'd come and slur his words so badly no one could hear what he was saying. And he'd want me to chat, and in those social situations, I just couldn't be swept up into the world of the little man.

I hope that didn't make him sad.

We always took city buses everywhere, or taxis. It occurs to me: Paul never learned to drive. He never had a driver's license. In a way, it was part of his management of his alcoholism; it would have been wrong to drive, he might have risked hurting someone.

So we waited for trolleys and buses and took them to Port Coquitlam especially and to Surrey and downtown and uptown. Or took taxis. Paul always paid in cash; he didn't use credit cards, only loan sharks.

Our neighbourhood was pretty quiet in those days with retired people, poor people on the other side of Main, families. At the bus stop heading down to the Hotel Ivanhoe for a drink from West 21st, in mid-afternoon, we'd often meet up with women who were mothers in the neighbourhood but who headed down to Hastings and Main in the late afternoon to work as prostitutes. Paul always greeted them and they chatted and me too if I knew them, and we asked after their kids.

The Downtown Eastside was deadly in those days but not that deadly, not like now.

But scary signs were there, like the corner store that sold only shoe polish and rubbing alcohol.

The Huron or Wendat are French-speaking; their own language is being recuperated now but in the little man's day it was pretty much wiped out. And his father had been a colonist in the 1930s in the Abitibi region from Montréal. It was a hellish experience for the majority of people, many of whom were left destitute after having been lured there by the Church teaching that it would be good if unemployed people went back to the soil. But it was a short growing season and the soil had to be first cleared of forest and they weren't farmers and the grip of the Church was absolute in their spiritual and economic lives.

8

Today I decided to research colonization in the Abitibi properly, as I also remember distant members of my own family by marriage whose family's health had been ruined by that colonization, and by the state and the Church conspiring to send the father to Québec City and incarcerate him in a mental institution there as insane, for insisting that people could make their own decisions about what to plant, or when to sell a cow, without asking permission from the curé. The state even charged him for the rail journey and for the policeman who accompanied him, and who stole the money out of his pocket as he slept. The authorities then took all his market-garden land for trumped-up "back taxes," though there were none owing; these tyrants were determined that the Rainas pay for the cost of the abduction, even if it left his family with only their house and no means of livelihood.

So many people in that family later died of TB. Anne Raina's older sister Clara had met my Uncle Harold in the Royal San in Ottawa, and I never knew this until I met Anne in

2010, and she told Clara's story to B. and me, and showed us photos. Now I think of Anne as my aunt; we are part of each other's family. Clara, her sister, recovered and lived to marry someone else after Uncle Harold, whom she knew as Harry, died on March 16, 1952 of leukemia as a result of the onerous treatments for TB. He contracted TB in the war, in a military training camp at Cornwall, Ontario, and was marshalled out as an invalid before even getting all his training, let alone fighting in the war. But he was a war casualty just the same, I think.

Anne Raina is now a fierce advocate in the fight against tuberculosis, and an advocate for the memories of those who doctored, nursed, housed, and exercised those who lived with tuberculosis after the war, as well as those people who lived with TB, and died of it, then and today.

She gave me black and white photos of Harry and Clara at the Royal Ottawa San, and at a picnic in the park. Before that, I'd only seen one photograph of Uncle Harold in my life, shown me by my Dad when I was a child. In that photo, Harry was lying in a bed at the San, on some kind of sun porch maybe. A ray of sun crossed the top of the metal frame of his bed. He died before I was born; it was a family tragedy. If you want, you can read Anne Raina's incredible book, *Clara's Rib: A True Story of a Young Girl Growing Up in a Tuberculosis Hospital*, and see Harry Moure there. On the Internet at anneraina.ca you can find more information and I recommend it; everyone should know about tuberculosis and its toll on human life.

Tuberculosis is on an upsurge again now, especially among the poor and badly housed, such as Indigenous populations in Canada's North. And in Nunavik in Québec. After three centuries of contact with European whalers and fishers, the tuberculosis bacillus arrived to Indigenous communities along with trading posts, flour, and metal cooking pans. And it's been up and down in Vancouver's Downtown Eastside as well. It wouldn't surprise me if Paul had TB on top of everything else that afflicted his lungs.

Suddenly I wish his cousin Betty had offered on the phone to save me one memory of him. I would have wished to have his health card from BC. Maybe it had a photo of him on it.

He was 5′ 7″ when I knew him and I was 5′ 11″. He wasn't one of those men unnerved by a tall woman; he was comfortable in his skin.

"Nothing could be finer, than dinner in the diner," the CN advertising jingle used to say. A lot of railway talk is rhymes like this. In Canadian English, it's railway, in American it's railroad. We always simply called it "the road."

The Vancouver train station had a huge neon sign along the top. The station was monumental and sat at the western continental end of the CN rail line, at False Creek, which was a small bay full of bobbing garbage back then.

There were people in the park outside the train station who drank anything, even shoe polish. Paul said he had once drunk shoe polish. You squeeze it through a cloth into a glass of water, or eat it on a piece of bread. Sometimes in the park under a tree behind a bush, you'd see a pile of empty shoe polish containers. Now those people were down and out. Men used up by logging or mining or other industries and cast out like spit into Thornton Park at the end of the railway by the sour weeds of False Creek. This was before the building of the SkyTrain. And before all the tall condominiums.

On the Internet I found an archival description of the Hildon Hotel, known first as the Manitoba Hotel, at 50 West Cordova, Paul's last home.

DESCRIPTION OF HISTORIC PLACE: The Manitoba Hotel is a six-storey glazed brick Edwardian commercial building on West Cordova Street near Carrall Street in Vancouver's historic Gastown area. Noted architect William Tuff Whiteway designed the Manitoba Hotel in 1909.
HERITAGE VALUE: This designated Edwardian hotel is associated with Gastown's history in the late nineteenth and early twentieth century as a mixed-use district, centre for Vancouver's trade and manufacturing. This type of hotel was in high demand to provide inexpensive housing for workers and to accommodate travelers and businessmen. This hotel and those like it in the immediate area contributed to the bustling street-level retail activity in the area. The historic value of this building also lies in its relationship to the surrounding neighbourhood and to adjacent buildings as part of the evolving streetscape. As did many others in Gastown, the Manitoba Hotel served a combined function

of providing commercial space on the ground floor for a wide range of tenants, and lodging and residential space on the upper floors. The building has been in continuous use for accommodation, as the Hotel Manitoba until 1954, and to the present as the Hildon Hotel. The building's classically-inspired Edwardian design, massing and scale speak to the period's evolving building technology, and to the shift in the social structure and economy that occurred at the turn of the century. Its height and simplified symmetrically-arranged facade of white brick typifies the change from the Victorian era and in this new form, evokes a major economic boom period in the west. — Source: City of Vancouver Heritage Conservation Program.

It's 3:30 p.m., and it's New Year's Eve now, December 31, 2015. Technically I should stop writing this tonight, as major holidays call a halt to shiva. I am not really ready to stop, though. And New Year's Eve depends on what calendar you are using.

As for me, I've just spent two hours looking up and down all the streets of Gastown on Google Street View in the hopes of finding Paul somewhere in Vancouver in May of 2015. I looked for a little man with a walker, his hair grey, well-dressed, his face pixellated, as Google does to protect people from being known. But I was sure I could recognize him by his body.

He wasn't there. I managed to make one good screen shot, though, looking up through the Google camera to the Hildon windows where, just behind the building, the sun is shining down, the little star.

That light, I think, is the little man.

There are two reviews of "The Bourbon Hotel" (the Hildon, misnamed for the bar at street level) on Google, both written by people with invented names. One from earlier in the fall of 2015 rates it 5-star (a joke) and says "I live here" as the reason. Ha ha. The second is from four years ago and says: "It is so drug infested. I wouldn't recommend renting it out to zoo animals. What a dump!!!!"

There's not enough visual information in the photo of the eight-month-old Paul on the balcony of the house in Montréal to identify where the building was located. But the little man always said he came from "No Damn Good," i.e., NDG, Notre-Dame-de-Grâce. In my day, it is a better neighbourhood than the one in which I live. In his day, it had a lot of working-class tenements along with better houses of immigrants getting a grip in this country at last. Its main street north–south was Décarie Boulevard, later made into a sunken expressway. The

building where his parents rented an apartment was expropri-
ated at that time, he had told me. Perhaps his house was on
Minto Avenue, a residential street between Addington and
Prud'homme that was flattened to make way for the Décarie
Expressway.

Minto Avenue doesn't exist now. I did find it on the Internet,
marked on an old aerial map in an article on trainyards and
vanishings.

On Décarie Boulevard there was a streetcar or tramway
you could take north to Belmont Park, a famed amusement
park on the Rivière des Prairies whose emblem of good
times was the balloon figure of the Laughing Fat Lady at the
entrance. It was a mythic park that among its rides held the
Cyclone, which until 1946 was the world's tallest and fastest
wooden roller coaster, on which riders in open cars sped down
the track at over 100 kilometres per hour. There were games,
freak shows, the ethos of the carney. Paul would have been
at home there. I found a photo of the Loop-O-Plane ride in
1943, the year he was born. It was kind of like the Hammer I
liked to ride at the Calgary Stampede with my brothers in the
1960s. Later on, the Belmont was deliberately targeted by the
city for any possible municipal infraction, to protect the city's
own amusement park, La Ronde, built on an island in the
other river, the St. Lawrence. Belmont Park closed down
the year before I came to Montréal.

There are condos today at Belmont Park. Still, the words
"Belmont Park" evoke magic. The little man would have gone

there with his parents and brother and sister on the streetcar from Minto Avenue, from the ancient Falaise de St. Jacques to the Rivière des Prairies, traversing the Island of Montréal.

Paul learned English in the streets of NDG.

Curiously, in one of my languages, Galician or Galego, "minto," the name of Paul's avenue that doesn't exist, is the first-person singular present-tense construction of the verb "to lie," i.e., to not be truthful. As in: to write things down. And you don't need to say "I" because you can tell by the verb declination who is speaking.

An Internet site called Closed Canadian Parks talks of Belmont Park. It says: "The 'Cyclone' roller coaster was installed in 1924. Designed & built by Herb Schmeck, H.F. Allen, and one of the Mitchell brothers, it lasted until 1983. The ride was apparently known as the 'Thriller' at some point, and in the early years as 'Montagnes Russes' and 'Scenic Railway.' It was built of coated British Columbia douglas fir on concrete footers, with steel cable reinforcement in high stress areas. The lift hill was 110 metres long, 19 metres high, and utilized a 75-horsepower motor. The L-shaped layout was 762 metres long with an 1143 mm track gauge and three block-brake runs. Part of it ran along the Rivière des Prairies. Each Philadelphia Toboggan train sat 24 riders in 3 four-bench, non-trailered cars with open fronts. Top speed was likely around 65 km/h . . .

"By the mid 1940s, along with the 'Cyclone' coaster and

carousel, were 17 other adult and kiddie rides . . . a walk-thru, a ballroom, shooting gallery, a photo gallery, and hand writing analysis. There were also midway games. And Fou-Rire, or Laughing Sal, in her red dress and painted lips, the famed figure at the entrance."

Further in Closed Canadian Parks, it says that one of the owners of Belmont Park during the 1930s was Charles-Émile Trudeau, whose son Pierre would become Canada's fifteenth Prime Minister in 1968. He would serve a total of fifteen and a half years in office. His son Justin is Canada's prime minister today. Justin Trudeau's name partly comes from "justice," and he says we owe it to ourselves to change our country's relationship with Indigenous peoples, which I know is absolutely essential, but a year after he has come to power, little progress has been made on fair funding of Indigenous education and on bringing clean drinking water to so many reserves.

The little man's middle name was Émile too. You always wonder what is and what is not an element of pure chance. There was a film made in 1957 at Belmont Park called *Pierrot à Montréal*. Pierrot loses his love, Columbine, to Harlequin, of course. You don't need English or French or any language to understand the film, as it is mimed. Oh Pierrot, the little man. You can still watch the film on the NFB website or app, and see even today what Belmont Park was like in the 1950s.

Giorgio Agamben, the Italian philosopher, in his book *L'usage des corps*, after the epigraphs, talks about the *corps d'usage*, which is not a body instrumentalized towards an end or production, but just the body used in and for itself. He asks how we might look at this body (which is also, says Aristotle, the body of the slave, one who has nothing) in order to wonder more deeply about taking action, and about happiness, in what we call a life.

I think about the little man and wonder if he was happy. I can't answer that question and yet I knew he was. Or, if not, I knew that he had felt happiness. Even as the fox of alcohol chewed out the inside of his body under his coat.

I don't know that the fox was joy, to tell you the truth. It was the churning thing that is our precious animal but that gorges itself on our muscle and spirit, no matter what. I have it too. So do you.

Blue Bonnets is another place of which the little man spoke to me. It was the racetrack in Montréal, partway up Décarie Boulevard on the tramway. Harness races started there in 1943, the year Paul was born. When I knew him he always preferred harness races, or "the ponies," to the thoroughbreds.

The little man loved the racetrack, and reading the racing forms of different colours, and analyzing the jockeys and horses and their statistics, and sitting outside in the breeze of the stands, and lining up below to go bet on the horses. Afterward, we would go inside and sit in the racetrack bar and have a drink and watch other racetracks on TV.

The earth dug out of Décarie Boulevard in 1965 to make the

Décarie Expressway was hauled to the St. Lawrence River and used to build St. Helen's Island for Expo 67, where La Ronde is today. In that way, the foundation of the little man's first Montréal home exists forever as amusement, and connects the past to now.

Amusement, though it is not happiness or joy, is, yes, a *usage du corps*. A fox.

In an article on the Internet, I found: "By contemporary standards, the Décarie Highway trench is a scar in the Island of Montréal. There have been implications on the physical, social and economic fabrics [of the city], such as [and] including socio-economic aspects, transportation, commercial and economic problems." It's a badly written sentence, but it's true about the scar.

For sure it was crap to have a sunken expressway open to the sky instead of a busy shopping street with a tramway whose line ended at a river and a park and a roller coaster.

My Mom also loved horses and the racetrack. I went with her a few times to the track in Vancouver, where Paul and I also used to go occasionally. I'd read the racing form as the little man had taught me, and bet my $2 until I'd lost $20, the maximum my Mom and I would each spend. My Mom didn't read the forms; she went to the paddock and looked at the horses then went to bet. She knew horses, she'd ridden one to school as a child. And horses knew her as well. She'd bet and always come away with a bit of money when the races were done (I usually ran out of my $20 about halfway through), and we'd get off the Hastings bus partway home and eat dinner in the Greek restaurant at Hastings and Clark. Now, from Google Maps, the restaurant seems to be called Yolks, but it still has the blue outside wall and columns of the Greek restaurant.

The outside décor had been kind of upscale in intention, at some point, but was tattered by the time my Mom and I used to eat there. The building was run as Conn's Cafe before the Second World War, started by someone's Greek grandfather. In the 1960s the café became the Greek Village, Vancouver's first truly Greek restaurant, catering to Greek seamen whose ships were berthed at the waterfront, and to Vancouverites who were just beginning to appreciate real Greek food.

The little man and I also ate there sometimes. Paul always had the lamb chops, *paidakia*, or the *kleftiko*, lamb stew.

It always seemed to me that NDG in Montréal, so English, was a strange neighbourhood for a francophone family to live, until I realized, looking at the map just now on the Internet, that the lower or southern part of NDG where the demolitions had occurred for the Décarie Expressway in fact almost adjoined the CP's Glen Yard, where Paul's father worked as a coach cleaner, i.e., a cleaner of passenger railway cars.

Paul never called himself Québécois, he called himself French-Canadian.

CP sold the Glen Yards in 2001 and the land was then decontaminated by removing upside-down mountains of earth. The MUHC Superhospital exists there now. It's the English hospital, but being as I am in the French system, the CHUM, I have never been there.

CHUM is MUHC backwards, just like "time" and "emit" are the same word in reverse. *Time emits*, I said that in an essay on translation, translations *emit*; they make time go backwards. And since all writing, to the reader, is a kind of translation, in reading, time can go backwards here too. The little man's story, thus, *emits*.

In our French system, we don't have a superhospital yet.

My research shows that the demolished residential streets nearby the Glen Yard were the east side of Addington, Minto Avenue, and the west side of Prud'homme. You could call them Minto Village. The 1962 city directory shows the area's residents to have been predominantly Italian in name.

Probably a lot of those men worked in the Glen alongside Paul's dad, I figure. Paul said that his first job was delivering beer for a corner store in his neighbourhood, on a bicycle with a huge basket on the front; then he went to work in a nightclub for Italians. Perhaps he met them in the neighbourhood where he'd grown. It was a lower middle class neighbourhood, by and large, but secure because the fathers had jobs and regular paycheques.

Minto was a one-sided street; the houses were only on the east side. On the west were the backs of the houses on Addington. The photo I have of the little man at eight months old on the balcony with his mother could be on the east side of the building in the morning sun. But maybe he lived on Addington or Prud'homme, as the light could be afternoon light. Baby Paul has a chubby belly; he had been well fed. Under the fold of his stomach is the proof that he's not wearing any diaper or clothes in the photo (these words clothe him, and the tender feeling I have on seeing the body of the baby who became the man with whom I lay years later in shared acts of love).

After the job with the nightclub, with *the Mafia*, as Paul called it (and said he was given a gun to carry for some of his jobs, though I was not sure I believed him, even before I knew what Minto Avenue meant), he took off to Halifax with some stolen money, spent it all, according to him, and then took the train all the way to Vancouver; his father had a CP pass that included his family, so he didn't have to pay. That would have been in the 1960s. I don't remember if the little man was in Montréal for Expo 67, or if he'd already gone.

It's strange that it's me who has lived in Montréal for thirty years now, longer than the little man ever did.

He had a girlfriend named Evelyn in Montréal, and when I met him he still had photos of her. She was slim and blond, and laughing. From the kitchen cupboards behind her, I could see that she had lived with him in that same basement suite in Vancouver. She had apparently followed him to Vancouver, or he had sent for her. My second name is Evelyn, after my grandmother Evelyn McCarthy, whose grandparents came to Québec in the nineteenth century from County Cork in Ireland during the famine, but maybe not because of the famine but because of some difficulties concerning loyalty to Ireland or to the Crown.

The little man said that, in Montréal while he was gone, Evelyn had come into trouble. She'd started to use drugs, I think it was, and perhaps, to prostitute herself to pay for them. The drugs made him sad, the necessity of them in her body. I don't think he related that history to his own with booze.

I don't remember why they broke up. He told me but I don't remember. I do remember that he told me years later that he'd had news that she had died. He was sad, I could tell.

I was his next girlfriend. I liked his ears and his sideburns and his hands. His voice and thoughts and the way he spoke. His gentlemanly demeanour, which fell hilariously but not completely apart when he was inebriated. He became like the

Little Tramp. Sort of seesaw wobbly and with a very serious expression, as if he hoped no one would notice.

Later, he wanted us to get married. He bothered me so much about it that finally I was worn down and said yes, and we did go to City Hall to get hitched but there was a garbage strike and the front door of city hall was locked and there were plastic bags of garbage piled against the door in protest. We couldn't find where to go and Paul got tired of looking and I never really did want to get married anyhow, and so we went to the Plaza 500 Hotel bar across from City Hall on Cambie Street and had a drink instead.

Actually it was the 1981 strike of civic workers in the CUPE union, which started in spring and lasted ninety days. Mike Harcourt was elected mayor later in November of that year, buoyed by CUPE and their supporters. A change was needed at City Hall.

We came to a sort of deal: we wouldn't get married but he could say we were married. Thus I became, at work, Mrs. Savard.

One time, coming home on Air Canada from Calgary or Toronto to Vancouver, I landed and I heard someone paging Mrs. Savard but didn't think it was me. When he found me waiting for my suitcase to arrive down the chute onto the conveyor belt, the little man was very angry. Why didn't you answer? he asked me.

I guess I never thought of myself as Mrs. Savard. And I thought of him as Mr. Angel, or Paul, or the little man.

Then there are the gifts he bought, small items of jewellery, though I rarely wear jewellery. There were, I remember, the crosses he bought me to travel with, the opals, and a small silver filigreed locket with his photo in it, on a silver chain. I went to Europe by myself in 1979 to travel in Greece, mostly, and he wanted me, as a single travelling woman, to be safe. And he thought that if some man bothered me, I could show him the cross and say "catholikos" or "καθολικός" and he would leave me alone.

It actually worked. And got me out of some bad-vibe situations.

I looked just now for a long time and did find one of the crosses still in a drawer, and the locket, though I know that the set of opals he bought me are now long gone.

Though the little man did not travel or want to, he sent me telegrams every few days, to my next stop, to tell me he loved me. I sent him postcards, which were, I am sure, destroyed by his cousin Betty in December 2015 after his death, as they would have been infested with bedbug eggs.

He didn't have very much chest hair but amid the hair that was there was one hair about two feet long. Every once in a while, he would uncurl it and stretch it out, amazed that it never received the message to stop growing. You should pull it out, I suggested. He was horrified. He'd curl it back up and nestle it in with the other hairs.

He always said hairs not hair. Comb your hairs! I am going to comb my hairs. In French, hair is always plural, *cheveux*. *Cheveu* is just one hair. In English one hair is a hair. Many hairs in English is just hair.

The Plaza 500 Hotel in Vancouver has been an empty high-rise for years now, apparently. When it was being renovated in 2011, black mould was discovered, and asbestos, and clumsy repairs led to uncertainty about earthquake stability. The authorities would only allow the workers to enter the building in hazmat suits and masks. Renovations came to a halt around that time, and some sources say that the owners stopped paying their bills.

9

It's New Year's Day, 2016. I've decided to keep writing for the full seven days of shiva, which will take me until January 3. Never mind that January 1 is a holiday. When I go to bed on January 3, I'll set my alarm for the early hours of morning on January 4, maybe 4:30 a.m. here in Montréal, which is 1:30 a.m. Vancouver time. I'll get up and light a candle for the little man, to mark the passage of one month since his death in the hospital in Vancouver.

I still see him as warm and comfortable and safe there. His heart was about to give out. He had difficulty breathing but maybe they had him on antibiotics for the pneumonia already, and had him on a mask so he could breathe more oxygen. The oxygen makes a funny quiet burble as it runs through the tubes from the wall or canister into the mask; it's right against your face and touches you, curiously a source of calm.

Probably the night shift started at 11 p.m. and the nursing staff went around at 11:30 p.m. to do the bed checks of all their patients. Paul would have been alive then. But when they went two hours later to do a check (probably they did one in between, too), Paul's vital signs were all at zero.

I don't like the word "flat-lining" though I know that that is what the monitor screen would have looked like. He had gone quietly. I think he knew he was being taken care of.

Of course I have no proof.

I can't possibly imagine the last time he might have thought of me. I did think of him in Calgary though, where I was helping B. with her struggles, and I had mailed him his Christmas card from there, very probably on the day he died.

The card wished him a year of good health and happiness in 2016. And called him an Old Goat, my old nickname for him.

Empire, York Street was dedicated in part to The Old G.

When coming home today on the bus from bringing B., still frail, to the Montréal airport for her return to Calgary after the holidays, I was thinking of Paul's teeth and of how often, because I have trouble with my own teeth (a bad occlusion), I have thought of those teeth of the little man. They were so worn in front. He grated his teeth at night so loudly that at times I could hear the noise of it. And the teeth were visibly wearing down.

I wonder how in his last years he managed to take care of his teeth.

I thought of another thing. When he lived in the basement suite at Tom's house, every year Paul would raise his own rent.

We'd walk to another restaurant as well, on Main at West 18th Avenue, in a little strip mall on the west side of the street. It was owned by a quiet couple who had infinite patience with Paul, and when he'd walk out without paying, they knew quietly that he'd be back the next day to settle his bill. They even learned to tell him they were out of Grand Marnier. I mean, I think they stopped stocking it forever so that he wouldn't stay and keep drinking after dinner. Yet Grand Marnier didn't even matter to him; I don't know why he was so fixated on it at that restaurant. I think it was called Mimi's. Maybe it was called Mimi's; I can't find any reference to it at all now on the Internet.

Finally he brought the owners a bottle of Grand Marnier as a sort of gift. I think they were horrified, as here was the Grand Marnier again.

10

It's been six days since I found out that Paul has died. I
spent today adding about 1000 words into the middle of the
text, mostly about Blue Bonnets Raceway and the Belmont
Amusement Park. The axis of the entire text, I think, is
Décarie Boulevard in Montréal in the 1940s and '50s, the
mime Pierrot, and the little man. Blue Bonnets Raceway
connects as well to Hastings Racecourse in Vancouver, where
we used to go see the races, Paul and me, my mother and me.
I don't think though that I ever went to Hastings Racecourse
with my mother and Paul. I was too afraid of his drinking,
and of being embarrassed in front of my Mom.

And all of it links to the Greek Village, the restaurant on
Hastings right where it bends at Clark, and the Hastings bus
goes by on its trolley wires.

We think we forget things but we do not. Agamben wrote that
responding to what is forgotten in us is an exigency, i.e., you
have to do it, to honour what is unforgettable. In his essay on
the epistle of the Apostle Paul to the Romans, there is a whole

part about memory. Agamben says: "Forgetting has a force and a way of operating that cannot be measured in the same terms as those of conscious memory, nor can it be accumulated like knowledge. Its persistence determines the status of all knowledge and understanding."

The film *Pierrot à Montréal* by Donald Ginsberg was made in 1957. It's on the NFB website and you can watch it and put yourself into the Belmont Park that the little man would have known as a teenager. Some days I think Paul was Pierrot, but also he was definitely Harlequin in the way he looked handsome and a bit *méchant*. Really, though, I think, he was the man with moustache, bowler hat and crooked bow tie, standing and watching from behind the main scene, the little man who worked for the Park putting up the numbers identifying the dance contestants when Columbine gets up to dance. That's the way I would like to remember him.

The plot and moving images go on around him, and he is just *there*, jaunty, enjoying the dance of the pretty young woman, enjoying her happiness. He doesn't know or care about the story, he just watches her as if she were a little star, shining for him.

Though, in a sense, I guess Paul is also the wiry man, also unnamed, who staggers after the crowd of men, at the point when Pierrot must fistfight the cocky Harlequin for his girl. He offers a glug from his mickey of *alcool* to the innocent Pierrot, who then fights all drunk in a comical scene that parodies a fight. This teetering man is dressed in ragged clothes, but the way he sways and looks, he too could be Paul.

Still, I prefer the idea that he is the little man running the dance contest, as that man has Paul's hands. His beautiful hands. And he looks at the young woman dancing with obvious delight in her dancing, yet not lasciviously, not like he's objectifying her. Just taking quiet pleasure in being alive in that very moment, his world made richer by the blurred twirling of the girl.

Sometimes it is the unknown ones who make our lives possible and make us draw in our breath at the magnificence of the world.

Tomorrow will be exactly one month from the day that Paul was admitted to St. Paul's Hospital. And then he died a few hours later. I need to think up a vigil. Maybe I will make *pâté chinois* with canned cream corn and a lot of allspice and cloves in the meat layer.

I decided to make the *pâté chinois* tonight, and eat it both days. Today, after all, it has been one month since Paul spent his last night in his home. The room in the Hildon Hotel.

I think suddenly that if he went to the hospital on December 3, it was because he did not want to die. He could have done the dying on his own in that room, 513. But he left somehow (ambulance, taxi?) and went to St. Paul's Emergency.

He wanted to live.

Children of the deceased may never sew the rent clothes, but any other mourner may mend the clothing thirty days after the burial. Shloshim. The Thirty Days.

Perhaps I am his child. I will never ever sew the clothes. Because there are not enough of us to mourn the little man. I don't want him to be ungrievable. I refuse to let this happen.

Now I'm crying a bit. The *pâté chinois* is in the oven. I made it the way he did as that is the way I always make it, just with less or no butter in the mashed potatoes. I have a trick (plain yoghurt and Polish mustard) that makes the potatoes taste rich without butter.

Before making it, I looked up all the recipes I could find online in French but none were like his. I can't make it any other way. He used to cook it on top of the stove and not in the oven, until the filling bubbled up around the potatoes for a while. I realized earlier, suddenly, thinking about this, that actually the oven in the stove in the basement suite at Tom's house did not work. It never worked.

I can fix stoves but Paul would not let me fix it. Funny that I only remembered this now.

I can start to smell the *pâté chinois* from my desk. You're supposed to grind up your own meat. One of the recipes I found online was in a PDF titled *Le pâté chinois — Trésor de la langue française au Québec*. I really like that. That the *pâté chinois* can be a treasure of the French language. Not just something to eat. It is the very language we speak.

In the newspaper *Le Devoir* in 2007, there was a long article about it. « Véritable plat de pauvre », dit Mme Bizier, le *pâté chinois*, dans sa forme originelle et quelques autres dérivés, va très vite s'imposer dans les cuisines, poussé par la crise économique et « les recettes de Jehane Benoît publiées dans les journaux invitant les gens à ne rien gaspiller », poursuit-elle. "A true dish of the poor," said Mrs. Bizier, "*pâté chinois*, in its original form and a few derivations, very quickly showed up in every kitchen, pushed by the economic crisis and the recipes of Jehane Benoît published in the daily paper inciting folks not to waste," she said. This· « plat de la débrouillardise » or "dish of sheer resourcefulness" is, in short, leftover meat (roast beef or pork) put through the grinder and placed between two layers of rice or under mashed potatoes, like the *hachis parmentier* of the French.

The corn came to the dish later, after the Second World

War, when someone named Onil Larose opened a canning factory to can the Québec corn his father grew. Then there was cream corn, and *voilà*, there it was in the *pâté chinois*. *Quand on le mange, on mange de l'appartenance sociale, de l'histoire.*

"When you eat it," the article says, "you eat social belonging, and history." You eat identity and nation. It is entirely a North American dish, not French, because of the corn. That would be right. I think the little man, French-Canadian, would agree with that.

As for the origin of the name, as a cook myself, I have my own version of that. But, as B. would say, I am not a professional or an expert, and so I will keep my opinion to myself.

When we were growing up, all our knowledge of Canadian cooking came from Madame Jehane Benoît and her show in the TV public affairs program *Take 30*, which ran from 1962 to 1984. She had written the major book of Québec cooking, then of Canadian cooking, then of microwave cooking, of which she became a devotee. We only knew that Canadian cooking came from Québec and was taught us by this rotund woman with a frilly apron. Madame Benoît. We spoke of her with reverence always.

I've made my own ketchup for the *pâté chinois*. And I'll eat it again tomorrow, reheated. It's delicious. It tastes like eating supper with the little man in a basement suite on West 21st in Vancouver, so many years ago.

The other dish I loved that Paul taught me to appreciate was kidneys, *les rognons*. I never have cooked them myself. It seems they take an initial blanching "to draw out the urine," as Paul said. On the Internet, it says that the kidneys' main function is to purify the blood by removing nitrogen-rich waste and funneling the waste into the urine. Another site says: "To reduce the strong flavour of beef kidneys, slice them and let them soak in cold water with a little added lemon juice or vinegar or salted cold water for two hours. You can also blanche them in boiled water with added vinegar or lemon juice for 20 minutes." I think they mean boiling water. That's what Paul did. Then he would sauté them in a pan with chopped onion and green pepper. They make their own gravy. Or perhaps he added mustard and cream, the standard French way of disguising kidneys, which is very delicious too.

When he'd do the blanching, I'd leave the house as I couldn't stand the smell. Offal. "Do not skip the presoaking step before cooking the beef kidneys, or the finished dish may have a strong, unpleasant flavor. If you don't have time to soak the kidneys for two hours, boil the pieces in water for several minutes and drain them thoroughly before cooking." That's from Livestrong.com. It also advises that kidneys are very high in cholesterol and may cause discomfort if eaten by those who suffer from gout.

I've rarely eaten them since, apart from a few times with Nicole Brossard at Chez Lévesque, that old French restaurant on Laurier Avenue, but I remember the feeling of happiness

95

when Paul decided to cook them. It must have been a recipe from his childhood, when offal parts were what poorer people most often ate. We in Calgary didn't eat kidneys, but we did eat liver, and we ate beef heart roasted and stuffed with bread stuffing and sewn shut with string. And tongue, also roasted. I really liked heart and tongue.

I haven't eaten them since.

Today is the seventh day of my honouring of Paul Émile Savard, man. That's what he accomplished in this life: he was a man. From the beginning to the end of his life, he was a man. When he was sober and walking down West Cordova or Hastings, or along West 21st, or down the aisles of a train car announcing dinner, he was a man. When he was slurring from the effects of alcohol on the human brain, and staggering, he was a man.

It was a hard enough job, I think, being this man. It didn't necessarily come to him naturally. I think naturally he would have been a field of high grasses with a high water-table and special small birds that needed both this grass and water. He would be the grass where the dew hits it and reflects glints of the sky.

He told me once that the most important thing about the sky, that most people forget or never acknowledge, is that it comes down to the ground. In fact the sky touches the ground. We don't have to look upward to be in the sky, we are always in it, it meets us and touches us.

The outlines of our bodies are always, always, touched by this sky.

I've never forgotten that.

His hands were angels' hands.

Today it's snowing a bit, from south to north, which is unusual, backwards. The entire roof of the rectory across the street, nestled in beside the stone of the nineteenth-century church, is now covered once more with snow. It's January 3. One month ago was December 3, 2015, which was the last full day on our Western Christian version of the human calendar that was lived completely by the little man.

I miss the little man. I haven't seen him for years, really, probably eight years at least, or ten. His sister Hélène was alive when I last saw him, and she died in 2010. When I was in Vancouver as resident writer at Green College last winter I didn't go down to the Eastside to find him. To tell the truth, I thought of him, and much of me wanted to go, but I knew I couldn't get myself mixed up in his problems, and in his ways in the world. I can't be around someone who drinks like that; it's bad for my mind.

I miss him being there, though, possible to find. I miss him walking up Main Street in Vancouver in my mind, with his beautiful slim hands in his coat so that he did not need gloves. I miss my Christmas card with the word "Paul" and his voice on the phone saying *Toots! Heh heh, you know who this is.*

I miss my memories of the little man, I want to say, which is why I am writing them down, as I don't want to lose my memories of him, of Paul Émile Savard.

For a week, I have been keeping his memory quietly alive each day, and touching the tear in my coat.

Inside my coat, where the fox of sadness is warmest, I feel it opening the ribs of my side to gnaw them.

I want to say too that the little man was brave.

I have no proof of this to offer, but I have to say it. He was brave.

He didn't shy from thinking of the sky and where it touched us. He said that god was breath and at the end he himself didn't have any. But even at the last moments of his life, the sky was touching him.

That was the world wherein lived the little man.

After leaving him in 1982, I went out briefly with only one other man. "Went out"; well I had sex with him one time. He was selfish, I thought. He was handsome but self-absorbed. I intended it as a kind of Paul cure, but what I found out was that not all men were like Paul.

The little man was never selfish. In any way.

Yesterday when I was walking along Duluth Avenue in Montréal in the snow, I passed the antique store run by the rude man and saw in the window a record cover of Dean Martin. I went back and took a photo of it through the glass with my phone. It reminded me of my mother's love of Dean Martin, of which I wrote in *Kapusta*, and the record had on it the title of the song that ends that book, "Volare." I can't quote the words here but I do refer readers to YouTube to listen to it on the Internet.

This is the photo I took. As I snapped it, I realize that the retouched and stylized Dean Martin, in this photo, looks quite like Paul Savard. Normally Dean Martin doesn't, really: his head is longer and more square, and his hair is actually parted on the other side.

The song titles on the album cover could be chapters of the life of the little man. "It's Easy to Remember," "I'm Yours," "Brother, Pour the Wine." On YouTube, at www.youtube.com/watch?v=svXxeaWwIno, you too can hear it: "You're Nobody 'Til Somebody Loves You."

And "Return to Me." Which holds those very words — *sorry, darling, if, hurt* — I had to walk away from to be sane.

But the little man was still a man, above all, trying to be a being-man. As Judith Butler mentions (echoing Deleuze, I guess), a man or human is only such because there is a beyond-human. This would be the grasses and sky that are also part of Paul. As are the bedbugs he would not have killed.

Dean Martin sang "Let It Snow": Paul used to sing the chorus of that song when it was snowing. He came from Montréal; he loved the snow. I still sing it too, and when I do, I think not of Dean Martin but of the little man.

Dean Martin also sang "That's Amore," which was my nickname on the railway. The clerical staff at Vancouver station would sing it to me, in a crazy chorus and to my utter consternation, in the crew office. Making fun of my last name, Moure, which is pronounced the same way as the last two syllables of "amore." But the moon as a pizza and all the shining and the too-much wine just embarassed me. Of course the crew clerks called me Mrs. Savard as well, out of respect for the little man.

Paul probably never watched anything on YouTube in his life. But he loved that old song of flying into the clouds, in Italian and English. That was Dean Martin, singing "Volare." It is what ends *Kapusta*, a book about being a daughter of my mother but also about genocide and our responsibility to speak up against intolerance that leads to genocide. Into the *cielo infinito*. Fly and sing. *Nel blu dipinto di blu*. Into that sky that touches us all.

It shakes me. Writing this and thinking about the little man this week has made me go more deeply into my own being; it's been crazier than a whole year of psychotherapy. I never made the connection until now: Dean Martin was my mother's favourite singer, whose show we used to watch on TV as children; we had to shut up when Dean was singing. He always had a drink or a "drink" and sometimes joked about drinking, and was always impeccably attired. And then I went away from home and fell in love with Paul, the image of my mother's TV boyfriend who made her feel more at home in America.

The Dean Martin Show, also known as the *Dean Martin Variety Show* for that's what it was, ran from 1965 to 1974 for 264 episodes. It was broadcast by NBC. In Canada it was on CTV, the second of our two TV stations, besides the CBC. The theme song to the show was Martin's 1964 hit, "Everybody Loves Somebody."

Dean Martin's second name was Paul. He died on Christmas Day in 1995, aged seventy-eight, of acute respiratory failure. Twenty years and two days before I learned of the death of Paul. He too had been a heavy smoker.

11

There are a few more things I have to say, and I have to say them today as January 3 is the final day I am writing.

I need to go back to Abitibi and read more about the colonization there in the 1930s. Failed colonizations hurt many and hurt families, and are part of a history that is still incorporated in human bodies, such as in that of Paul Émile Savard.

I found one article on the Internet that talks about the disappointment and shattered dreams of those French-Canadians who went to the Abitibi. "The Catholic Church," it says, "played a key role in promoting and organizing the colonization. . . . The theme it developed was that of the return to the land as a plan of salvation for the French-Canadian nation. *Plan of salvation* meant avoiding the waste and corruption that was rife in the cities and it also meant the cult of poverty and misery, not for the Church of course, but for the flock, that is to say the population of the colony."* The article

---

* « L'église catholique a joué un grand rôle pour promouvoir et

is in the Marxist–Leninist newsletter *Chantier Politique* from September 23, 2013 so you may reject it but what it says — and there's more there on the control of the Church over every aspect of life, whether political, economic, or religious — reflects the way Paul spoke of what had happened. Though he spoke little of it, and knew little of it, as he was small or not yet born.

Judith Butler says on page 119 of *Towards a Performative Theory of Assembly*: "Every political effort to manage populations involves a tactical distribution of precarity, more often than not articulated through an unequal distribution of precarity, one that depends upon dominant norms regarding whose life is grievable and worth protecting and whose life is ungrievable, or marginally or episodically grievable, and so, in that sense, already lost in part or in whole, and thus less worthy of protection and sustenance."

I marked this quote and in the margin of the book I wrote, simply, in pencil: "Paul."

I refuse now and forever to let the life of the little man be ungrievable.

There is another Butler quote I would like to say here. It

---

organiser la colonisation . . . Le thème qu'elle a développé c'est celui du retour à la terre comme planche de salut pour ce qu'elle appelaient la nation canadienne-française. Planche de salut voulait dire éviter la déperdition et la corruption qui sévissait dans les villes et cela voulait dire aussi le culte de la pauvreté et de la misère, pas pour l'église évidemment, mais pour les ouailles, c'est-à-dire la population de la colonie. »

comes from the next page: "When any of us are affected by the sufferings of others, it is not only that we put ourselves in their place or that they usurp our own place; perhaps it is the moment in which a certain chiasmic link comes to the fore and I become somehow implicated in lives that are clearly not the same as my own. And this happens even when we do not know the names of those who make their appeal to us or when we struggle to pronounce the name or to speak in a language we have never learned."

I don't think Paul suffered. He wasn't anywhere where there were bombs or huge hurts. I hope he didn't suffer. Not being able to breathe, though, is no fun. You want to die when you can't breathe.

But Paul went to the hospital. He wanted to live.

Maybe some of his friends or neighbours in the Hildon Hotel helped him into a taxi. All the way down five flights of stairs. Or maybe he was getting home from somewhere else and went through the door of the Hildon and could no longer go up the stairs. Because of his breathing.

With him, I took a lot of taxis, yellow and black ones, Black Top they were called. From bars back then you could ask the waiter to call you a taxi. Or there was a taxi phone near the street door of the bar, linking you directly to the dispatcher.

The Internet says that in rhetoric, which I have always liked, chiasmus "(Latin term from Greek χίασμα, 'crossing,' from the Greek χιάζω, chiázō, 'to shape like the letter X') is the figure of speech in which two or more clauses are related to each other through a reversal of structures in order to make a larger point; that is, the clauses display inverted parallelism."

It is the point in life at which in language you can cross over into another's life and touch it like a sky.

This text is chiasmic. I just thought I'd say.

After we'd broken up and I'd moved into a co-op to have better accommodation away from the apartment next to the fire station (where I had already moved all my clothes to the space I was using as my office), I started to reconstruct my life. I joined the maintenance committee and learned about steam heating, and about Robert's Rules of Order. Sometimes people would let Paul in the front door of View Court Co-op and I would come home and find him sitting in front of my apartment door with a case of beer, opening the bottles with his teeth. I had always to send him away; I would see him, but not when he was drinking and not in any situation where there would be alcohol.

Then we almost reconciled long-distance in the summer of 1982. Paul was in Montréal visiting his parents and sister and niece on Île Perrot where by then they lived comfortably. He phoned me to ask if we could try again. I said I would think about it, wanting to get him off the phone. I did think about it and remembered going to City Hall during the garbage strike to get married then not getting married. I felt I should try again. Paul phoned back to try to convince me and I didn't believe his promises, but I felt responsible before the forces of the universe and sky, and agreed to meet him at the airport when he came home, and discuss trying again. It was to be a symbol: Montréal and Vancouver; the planes and arrivals, the history of the Savard family in Québec and, at this end, me in Vancouver, that's Amore.

Two or three weeks went by with Paul still in Montréal, and there came a day when I had to admit to myself I'd fallen in love with the future paleontologist who lived in my co-op building who was at that time a photographer, and I was ready to admit a desire that I had never been able until then to admit, and come out as a lesbian.

The result was that I didn't go to the Vancouver airport when the little man's vacation ended. He was very upset and disappointed. I couldn't help disappointing him but I wished it didn't have to be so dramatic and involve the airport. Once back in the basement suite, Paul phoned me to insist that I reconsider, and that I see him. He came to my house very upset that I'd not been at the airport, and upset at my phone conversation with him, and wanting to convince me to come back to him.

He'd never before come over to my house in a business suit. He was very serious and honourable, like an undertaker, almost, and he wanted his seriousness to be known in the comportment of his body, and in his attire.

I had to tell him I was in love with a woman and we could be friends but that was it. We just stood in my apartment without sitting or even moving, he shorter and impeccable and me taller, the walls of the small room valiantly holding the sky at arm's length so it would not graze our bodies for the time that we spoke.

In the end, he loved me enough to believe me and he grew to accept this change of plan.

After that, he used to come over to play cribbage or backgammon and sometimes he'd buy three theatre tickets and invite the three of us out together. My new love often demurred as Paul was a heavy smoker and it wasn't appealing to her, and also, she didn't like playing cribbage or hearts.

We used to play a lot of cribbage, backgammon, and hearts back at the kitchen table in the basement suite at 15 West 21st, and in the Legion, which was really the Army, Navy and Air Force Veterans Taurus Branch 298 at 23rd and Main. We'd play shuffleboard too, at a really rundown hotel on Cordova whose name I can't even find any more. But they had the smoothest shuffleboard. Paul was good at the shots; he watched curling on TV and it was similar but smaller, and he knew all the rules.

I still wonder about the word "was," the word "is," the word "knew."

At the gym the other day in Montréal, there was a curling match on the TV screens, and on the scoreboard displayed over the action, the team skipped by "Gushue" had a little hammer beside its name. Because of Paul, even all these years later, I know that this means his team would throw the last rock of the end. "He's got the hammer," we'd say. It's a chance to change the course of the game forever.

In the co-op, we just played cards, Paul and I. Cribbage or hearts. That is what people do when they are not working or eating and there is no television. My new partner would go develop her incredible photographs in the red darkness of another apartment in the same building.

I really can't find the name of that hotel on Cordova with the shuffleboard and when I tried to think of whom I could call who would know, I thought of Paul, of course.

Well, forget that, then.

I have this creeping feeling that it might actually have been the Hildon Hotel.

Curiously, Paul is the reason why I have always slept on the side of the bed I do. I can't remember why it was that I ended up or chose the side I slept on, but the little man was part of it. I kept on ever afterward and still do, always sleeping on the same side of the bed.

12

I have to get back to the Abitibi; the clock is ticking; it is getting dark in Montréal so there are not more than three hours of light left in Vancouver either. A month ago, in the chiasmus of time's crossing, the little man is seeing his last light of earth.

Shine on me, little star.

One sees that last light without ever knowing it's the last.

Judith Butler ends her chapter on page 122, saying, and I shorten: "We struggle in, from, and against precarity. Thus, it is not from pervasive love for humanity or a pure desire for peace that we strive to live together. We live together because we have no choice, and though we sometimes rail against that unchosen condition, we remain obligated to struggle to affirm the ultimate value of that unchosen social world . . . We can be alive or dead to the sufferings of others — they can be dead or alive to us. But it is only when we understand that what happens there also happens here, and that 'here' is already an elsewhere, and necessarily so, that we stand a chance of grasping the difficult and shifting global connections in ways that let us know the transport and the constraint of what we might still call ethics."

The chapter ends on that word, ethics. I think it is that word I contemplate when I contemplate Paul, and maybe knowing him in some way has made me capable of this contemplation. As well as capable of understanding precarity in a different way than anyone of privilege can understand it. And we are all, me, Butler, you perhaps, people of privilege.

Butler disagrees with Agamben about his idea of bare life but I think she misreads it. It's not the place to go into it here, and I don't really have a right to object, but I just want it noted. In *Means Without Ends*, Agamben does talk about *zoë*, bare life, as the simple fact of being-alive. He goes on to criticize his own term, I think, when he says: "With the term *forme-de-vie* we understand, on the contrary, a life that can never be separated from its form, a life of / in which it is never possible to isolate something like a bare life."

The simple fact of being-alive meant everything to Paul, but even so, it is not possible to isolate in his form-of-life, a bare life. That seems right to me.

My aunt Anne's sister Mary Elizabeth Raina, also a writer, wrote *We Have Written: A True Story About Our Struggle to Maintain Dignity in the Face of Oppression* and published it herself. The Rainas are kind of fierce about self-publishing.

They get their books to the public without the confused intermediary of the publishing house, which so often discards what is new and valuable out of fear masked as "marketability," and publishes only what is the same.

Mary's book recounts the experience of the Raina family in the Abitibi as colonists at Saint Marc de Figuery, sixteen kilometres south of Amos, Québec, on the road to the mines at Val d'Or. On November 28, 1932, the Raina family arrived there from Western Canada. Dominic Raina, the father, had taken his family from a successful farm in Alberta to avoid the dustbowl of the Depression and start a new life where they could learn French and be Catholic, under the auspices of a federal colonization program linked with Québec's. By 1934, the oppression of the local curé and the resulting censure of the family and of Dominic's views of democracy in local government — as necessarily involving the people and the views of all — was such that he wished to take his family away. The curé instead conspired, in the name of the One, Holy, Catholic, and Apostolic Church and with the cooperation of the local doctor and police, to have Dominic Raina abducted so as to incarcerate him as insane in the asylum in Québec City, the *Asile Saint-Michel-Archange*. First the local police came and took him from his home, and threw him in the local calaboose and then the doctor, a medical doctor who had sworn the oath of Hippocrates to do no harm, came and gave Dominic an injection right through his clothes to put him to sleep so that he could be hoisted onto the train to Québec City.

Mary Raina's book is about the oppression perpetrated by

the Church in the northern village of Saint Marc de Figuery during that colonization, which was partly advertised and sponsored by the Church and also by the federal and provincial governments, who sought ways to wiggle out of supporting urban families devastated by the Depression and shipped them instead to colonize the north for the exploitation of mines and forests, to "save the nation" as French and Catholic. Not one of the authorities asked the Atikamekw, Abitibiwinni, Ojibwe and Cree peoples, whose land it was from time immemorial, what they thought.

I don't know about that oath of Hippocrates. Too often, it seems to get mixed up with hypocrites. I'm thinking here of a poetry critic who was also a medical doctor, who wished a long time ago in a public interview that people be allergic to my poetry. He had a reputation for compassion, but I don't know if wishing allergies, which can be so perilous and painful in daily life, on humans is consistent with an oath to do no harm.

One of the proofs used retrospectively by the curé of Saint Marc de Figuery to demonstrate to his parishioners that Dominic Raina, their neighbour, was insane was a letter Dominic had written from the asylum in Québec City to his family. Only an insane person would use both English and French in the same letter, the priest said. Which makes me and even la plupart de mes amies insane.

Even the village mail was opened by this curé before being delivered, it seems. Today, there is a street in Saint Marc de

Figuery named after the curé Jules Michaud. There is nothing named after the farmer and democrat Dominic Raina.

The municipal plan for the town, in its current descriptive publication, praises this curé as a man in favour of the town's development. Clearly capitalism and the Church and oppression were all one and the same thing, along with the oppression and exclusion of the Abitibiwinnik. The document says: "The man who drove the development of the community was the priest Jules Michaud, appointed to the parish in 1926. He organized the construction of the current church in 1928. The church was finished in December of that year, in time to celebrate 'midnight mass.' He was also cashier and manager of the credit union as well as being active in most of the organizations in the community."*

I think of the darkness at the hospital and Paul at rest; probably there were three other persons in beds in the room with Paul. I've forgotten to think of them, and were they sleeping, and did their human presence help give the little man the calm to let go of the ache of breathing in the near-dark, lit only by quiet machines?

---

* « L'homme qui stimula le développement de la communauté est le curé Jules Michaud. Il devient le curé de la paroisse en 1926. Il met rapidement en marche le chantier de la construction de l'église actuelle qui débute en 1928. Elle est complétée pour décembre pour y célébrer la « messe de minuit ». Il sera caissier et gérant de la Caisse Populaire en plus d'être actif au sein la majorité des organismes de la municipalité. » English translation is by our author.

Earlier, before the colonizations, between 1914 and 1917 at the Spirit Lake Internment Camp near Saint Marc de Figuery, Canadian families with Ukrainian-born parents were interned under the War Measures Act, as they were considered citizens of Austria, with which Canada was at war. Although it is true their native soil in Europe lay in lands then ruled by the Austro-Hungarian Empire, they were far from considering themselves Austrian, and many were Canadian born. But Canada removed their rights and took their property, and interned them as enemy aliens in the north of Québec, and in other places, such as the Rockies near where I grew up, at Castle Mountain. As children we were brought there on walks by our mother, looking for remnants of barbed wire or wood or brick on a flattened area, overgrown. She told us prisoners were kept there. Their crime was simply having been born in one place instead of another, and then having gone somewhere else.

Between 1915 and 1917 in northern Québec, Spirit Lake's prisoners, which included sixty families, cleared more than 500 acres of forest. They were paid twenty-five cents a day and, as one resident who built bunk houses for the internees recalls, they were fed "cabbage, cabbage and more cabbage." Today the same place is called Lake Beauchamp, the call to the spirit having been erased. The Internment of Persons of Ukrainian Origin Recognition Act, Bill C–331, in which Parliament "expressed its deep sorrow for these events" but did not apologize, was given royal assent in November 2005, signed into law almost ninety years later.

Following this, on May 9, 2008 the Canadian government

established a $10 million fund held in trust by the Ukrainian Canadian Foundation of Taras Shevchenko. The interest earned by this fund goes to support projects that commemorate the experience of thousands of Ukrainians and other Europeans interned between 1914 and 1920 and the many others who suffered a suspension of their civil liberties and freedoms. No fund, however, represents the francophones of Québec and the families of other origins who were subject to oppressions in that area too. No fund recognizes the dispossession of the Abitibiwinnik.

Having gathered these fragments, I will not tell that whole story here, for I cannot. I just want to say that I have long known from Paul that the terrain and life in the Abitibi were not necessarily happy for the urban colonists urged there from Montréal.

I wonder about the heart and lungs of the little man, slowing in a warm and clean room as night announced the coming of a new day, and I think about the increasing space between his breaths, and about the very last breath he will take, his alveoli that absorb breath as oxygen into the blood still and finally touching all of the sky. It must be exactly a month ago now.

Really, I know nothing of the Savard family's stay in the Abitibi, only that they went there via the One, Holy, Catholic, and Apostolic Church to be colonists and own land, and that it broke them and they returned with nothing to Montréal, possibly before Paul Émile was born.

One of the colonizing booklets of the era, written by another curé, l'Abbé Beauchamp, for whom Spirit Lake was renamed, fulminated: "Our sons who live afar, in the USA, in Ontario, in the Western Provinces, threatened constantly by the common enemy, can say to their adversaries: 'In opposing our free expansion, in restraining our freedoms, our rights, you work against your own interests, you block a source of moral, social and economic progress. These same institutions that you stop from growing, look what they have achieved in Québec. Québec is, in effect, at the head of confederation.'"*

It referred to the expansion of the Catholic Church and the production of large French-speaking families living in pious servitude to the curé and the policeman on unceded Abitibiwinni lands.

In just one year, 1932–1933, 488 families established themselves in Abitibi-Témiscaming in accordance with the Gordon Plan, named after the federal Minister of Employment. This plan offered $600 every two years to each head of family who accepted to be a colonist and return to the land and clear it. Unfortunately, these father-heads were mostly not prepared

---

* « Il est nécessaire que les fils qui vivent au loin, aux Etats-Unis, dans l'Ontario, dans les provinces de l'Ouest, sans cesse menacés par l'ennemi commun, puissent dire à leurs adversaires : "En vous opposant à notre libre expansion, en restreignant nos libertés, nos droits, vous travaillez contre vos propres intérêts, vous tarissez une source de progrès, non seulement dans l'ordre moral, mais aussi dans l'ordre social et même économique. Ces mêmes institutions que vous empêchez de naître ou de grandir, regardez ce qu'elles ont accompli dans le Québec. Québec est, en effet, à la tête de la Confédération." » Translation into English by Toots, our author.

for their new role nor for the brutal challenges of clearing land and farming. The difficulties caused almost a third of the families to return south to the city within two years.

"Most of the aspiring colonists from the cities, chosen to return to the earth, were extremely poor. All were unemployed, on welfare or employed by the municipality at the time in a work program for the unemployed. . . . Many had not paid their rent for several months. A journalist saw fit to call these unfortunates 'a band of ragged beggars oozing misery.' "*

Those who abandoned the colony in penury to return south to the city on the great *fleuve* were treated as wasters of money and irresponsible, above all those young couples — 60% of those who abandoned the north — who had not yet any children and thus lacked family responsibilities. Instead of remaining in the bosom of the Church and its dream of colonization, they followed the bad advice of family and friends and returned, as did Yvan Savard, to Montréal.

And so I have a picture of an infant little man on a wooden balcony on a street that no longer exists, or that exists invisibly in the sky just above a sunken expressway, the eldest son of a

---

* « La plupart des aspirants-colons des villes, choisis pour le retour à la terre, étaient d'une extrême pauvreté. Tous étaient des chômeurs, sous les secours directs ou employés par les Municipalités de temps autre pour travaux de chômage. . . . Plusieurs n'avaient pas payé leur loyer depuis plusieurs mois. Un journaliste s'est plu appeler ces malheureux "une bande de gueux déguenillés et suintant la misère" ».

father who no longer exists who worked in a trainyard that no longer exists.

The little man is sitting and smiling and his mother is wearing a beautiful summer dress in 1944. I want his smile to exist forever.

Despite the peaceful stillness of the domestic scene, the Second World War was still raging, though more than likely (from the sun and the little man's nakedness) the photo was taken after D–Day in June of that year, when, in a second wave of landings in Normandy at Bernières-sur-Mer, the riflemen of the Québec-based Régiment de la Chaudière waded ashore, to the surprise of locals, says the Internet, who were amazed to be addressed by soldiers of the liberating forces in their own tongue.

It took until 1962 to rebuild the city of Caen, destroyed by bombs and fighting in the Liberation; nothing now remains of its medieval history. Young Clara Raina did make it out of the Royal Ottawa San, cured of tuberculosis, in late 1952; she'd been there from the age of twelve to twenty-six. On January 5, 1953, my Uncle Dick wrote from 122 Pamilla Street in Ottawa (the house still exists) to his brother my Dad, who was in the RCAF and lived at 420 Edmonton Street in Winnipeg (which doesn't), saying: "Clara Raina is home at last, condition good." Clara lived to fall in love again and marry another Harry, who had fought at Caen in the war. My aunt Anne said that the experience of war affected him forever.

I touch Paul's cheek with my words, words I cannot even

write here, for my mouth wants to ache with them all alone. I can see his well-trimmed shock of grey hair, which had never thinned. I think of his serious-eyed smile, which was always the smile of the baby seated with its mother on the hot planks of the summer balcony in NDG.

One of my old nicknames from the time we spent together is Ruin E. Rome, an anagram of my name, invented by my friend Marianne, who also knew the little man. I actually think it was her who first named him "the little man."

Rome is the home of Catholicism, of course, and of its pope who this year is Argentinean and makes pleas for consideration toward those who live in precarity. Rome is also the city where the German poet Rainer Maria Rilke wrote many of his iconic *Letters to a Young Poet*, including number 7, which argues for a conception of love other than the conventional one of man and woman. The letter speaks eloquently of this different love and contains these thoughts:

"This more human love (a love infinitely considerate and quiet) is one which we prepare painfully and with struggle, so that two solitudes may protect, border, and greet each other."

After writing the letter, Rilke will lift his head from words and turn back to the present tense of Rome, I guess. Maybe he goes for a walk or maybe just shuts off the light and goes to sleep. He closes his letter first, though, by saying something which, I think, rings true for me and the little man. Paul was older than me but we were both so young.

All of this happened a long time ago.

At the end of Letter 7, Rilke writes: "I believe that this love so strong and powerful will remain in your memory because it was your first deep aloneness and the first inner work that you had done in your life."

Last Sky for the Little Man

For Paul, this day one month ago was his final experience of light from the sky. After night fell on his December 3, he never saw daylight again.

Only the little star shone, outside his hospital window.

I've got my *pâté chinois* to eat tonight to honour him as it is his recipe forever, and I will light candles to keep vigil with him on this eve of the day of Shloshim. I'll go to bed early as usual in Montréal but will set my alarm for 1:30 a.m. Vancouver time and get up and maybe play a song of Dean Martin's on YouTube. Maybe someone like the little man can't get old; he always has to stay the King of Cool.

Of course I'm exaggerating.

Paul didn't care about being cool. He was the man who took delight in what happened in front of him. That's how

I remember him. He's the Artistotelian man whose life is neither praxis nor poeisis; it was a form of being alive not yet accounted for by any of the current definitions of work, production, accumulation, market, success.

I know he went to the hospital to live. To die wanting to live is an act of bravery.

I told you: the little man was brave.

I'm trying to make myself feel better, I know, because I will never see the little man, the Old Goat, P.E. Savard, again, and I will never again hear his voice saying *Toots* on the phone. *Hey Toots, heh heh heh.*

Maybe when I get up in the night after midnight to honour the moment of his leaving the earth one month ago at 1:30 a.m. PST on December 4, 2015, I'll play Dean Martin singing "I Still Get a Thrill" in 1950. It's right here at www.youtube.com/watch?v=A-vLCY1vSXk.

Or maybe I'll just sit up in bed and call his name, Paul Émile Savard, into the sky. I won't have to say it very loud because the sky already touches me. It even goes inside my mouth to touch my tongue where I am speaking.

His name and that sky and the shining of the little star.

Bye Paul.

Bye forever, Paul.

星

I don't want to let you go, I don't want this to be the last line.

But it must be so.

love,
Toots

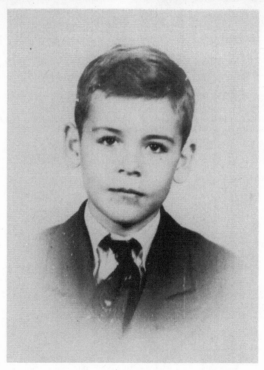

TOP: Queen
Elizabeth Park
cafeteria, April 1978.
LEFT: Vancouver,
VIA Rail,
September 1980

Paul and MIM, October 1980, YVR.

Still from *Pierrot in Montreal* ©1957 National Film Board of Canada. All rights reserved.

PULLING THROUGH
for Paul

Sometimes the invisible pulls
all its blankets away from us.
If only it would stop.
Last night, i saw you on the lake pulling
your brother thru a hole in the ice.
What lake, you say.
From grey water into your arms, the familiar
greeting between brothers, between
good men.
Snow pounded around you, ridiculous
image of white,
skies open like a grey bird, & you moving.
Whole forests of words.
You always wanted to leave like this,
the city & its stalled seasons, leave Main Street
& build a house somewhere, or in Hope.
Dommage, dommage, but in my dream there were
no houses, only you & your brother & the monstrous
dance of winter, now —

you are singing, your brother
stiff w/ cold, still in your embrace; you are remembering
a whole childhood to him, together,
kissing his shocked head.
Into his ear you feed twenty-year old bread, old doorways,
sour rats, a continent, more & more cabbages!
Finally he nods, mouth twisted open to laugh, his hand

clenched upon yours: he pulls
your arm, rowing it wildly —
he takes you w/ him
across the ice, rowing your faint lives, gladly, like brothers!

Erin Mouré, age 24
from Empire, York Street *(Toronto: House of Anansi, 1979)*

Readings and Google Traces (Acknowledgements)

This is a creative-critical work: a memoir by a biased party and thus a work of the imagination, a work of cellular compulsion and psychic keening, which turned out to be a work of social history. It is an assemblage and pastiche, created by a mind in grief struggling for words of its own, trying to record old memories, and holding them together by obsessive and lonely Google searches for events and acts that now no one can know, to protect these things for future humans in search of someone and something they too cannot and will not find ever again.

I thank all the authors and providers of works on the internet in all their variety, and if I have failed to credit someone, please contact the publisher and it will be rectified in any future edition.

Cover: Detail from "Ovaltine Café" by Greg Girard, in *Under Vancouver: 1972–1982*, Toronto: The Magenta Foundation, 2017. Used by permission. The street it depicts is East Hastings, in Vancouver's Downtown Eastside, just at the edge of Chinatown.

p. vii: Judith Butler, *Notes Toward a Performative Theory of Assembly*, Cambridge, MA: Harvard U Press, 2015, 197.

p. viii-ix: Giorgio Agamben, *L'usage des corps*, trans. Joël Gayraud. Paris: Seuil, 2014, 16; and *The Use of Bodies*, trans. Adam Kotsko, Stanford CA: Stanford U Press, 2016, 16.

p. 3:   For an overview of the history of education in Québec, see: Mathieu Pigeon, "Education in Québec, before and after the Parent reform" at collections.musee-mccord.qc.ca/scripts/explore. php?Lang=1&tableid=11&elementid=107__true&contentlong

p. 3:   On the Downtown Eastside (DTES) of Vancouver, from a 2014 City of Vancouver planning document, http://council.vancouver. ca/20140312/documents/cfsc5.PDF :

> With some of Vancouver's oldest neighbourhoods and the historic heart of the city, the DTES has a unique and diverse character, with mixed income residents living in several areas that are rich in history. The DTES is also strongly connected to its founding Aboriginal communities (including the Musqueam [xʷməθkʷəẏəm], Tsleil-Wauthuth [mi ce:p kʷətxʷiləm] and Squamish [Skwxwú7mesh] First Nations), Japanese Canadians, Chinese Canadians, and other ethnic and cultural groups. The uniqueness of DTES also stems from the early settlements in the areas of Gastown, Powell Street (Japantown), Oppenheimer, Chinatown and Strathcona, with their distinctive low- to medium-rise buildings and smaller scale architecture linked to the diverse communities and their cultural aspirations over time. The DTES is located on land that Aboriginal communities consider unceded Coast Salish territory and has been the urban home of many Aboriginal communities for generations. Many elements of Canadian history are rooted in the diverse communities of the DTES — the Chinese Head Tax, the forced displacement and internment of the Japanese Canadian community during World War II, the displacement of First Nations and the residential school policy.
>
> The community has considerable diversity; there are working poor and middle income families, couples and singles of all ages living in a range of housing. Residents are proud and value the sense of belonging and feelings of acceptance experienced in the area, and many struggle with complex challenges, including homelessness and affordable housing, unemployment, physical disabilities, addictions, and mental health issues. The area has numerous non-profit organizations, service agencies, and community groups offering critical support to these communities.

p. 11:   Erín Moure, "Pulling Thru," *Empire, York Street*. Toronto: Anansi, 1979, 61.

p. 13:   On Notre Dame de Lorette: www.ndlorette.ca/
         historique.php

p. 14:   On Serge Savard: www.ourhistory.canadiens.com/player/
         Serge-Savard

p. 20:   John Heywood, *A dialogue conteinyng the nomber in effect of all
         the prouerbes in the englishe tongue compacte in a matter concernyng
         two maner of mariages, made and set foorth by Iohn Heywood.*
         London: Thomas Berthelet, 1546. (http://name.umdl.umich.edu/
         A03168.0001.001)

p. 22:   Erín Moure, *Pillage Laud*. Toronto: BookThug, 2011, 9.

p. 22:   Antonio Tabucchi, *Les trois derniers jours de Fernando Pessoa, un
         délire*. transl. Jean-Paul Manganaro. Paris: Seuil, 1994.

p. 23:   On Denis Marleau, and his stage adaptation: www.thecanadian
         encyclopedia.ca/en/article/denis-marleau and http://ubucc.ca/
         creation/les-trois-derniers-jours-de-fernando-pessoa

p. 24:   On VIA Rail: www.wikipedia.org/wiki/Via_Rail

p. 25:   Toots's claim that her phrase with "this great land" is part of a
         song might be an oblique reference to Gordon Lightfoot's "Canadian
         Railroad Trilogy," from 1967, though Toots's phrase is just a normal
         Canadian sentence and not a song lyric at all, and not a quote from
         Gordon Lightfoot.

p. 29:   On porterhouse steak: www.wikipedia.org/wiki/
         porterhouse_steak

p. 30:   Erin Mouré, "Tricks," *Wanted Alive*. Toronto: Anansi, 1983, 35.

p. 30:   On Woodwards: www.wikipedia.org/wiki/Woodwards

p. 31:   On Restricted Life Income Funds: www.osfi-bsif.gc.ca/Eng/
         pp-rr/faq/Pages/lif-frv.aspx

p. 34:   On bedbugs: www.bedbugregistry.com/location/BC/V6B/
          Vancouver/50%20W%20Cordova%20St

p. 36:   On Abbott Mansions: www.changingvancouver.
          wordpress.com/2015/11/19/abbott-mansions-west-hastings-and-
          abbott-se and www.centralcityfoundation.ca/our-impact

p. 39:   On cigarettes: www.wikipedia.org/wiki/Rothmans,_Benson_
          &_Hedges

          On the views of Philip Morris International: www.pmi.com/
          our-business/about-us/our-views/health-effects-of-smoking-tobacco

p. 43:   Rabbi Maurice Laam on shiva in the Jewish tradition: www.
          aish.com/jl/l/dam/48956706.html. The quotes from Rabbi Yisrael
          Rutman are at www.aish.com/jl/l/dam/48961211.html

p. 45:   Mia Stainsby, "A Lingering Taste of 10 Memorable Eating
          Spots," *Vancouver Sun*, April 16, 2011: www.vancouversun.com/
          news/vancouver-125/lingering+taste+memorable+eating+
          spots/4625211/story.html

p. 45:   Robert Boyd, "Two Survivors: a Seafood Place and Old Neon,"
          from canadianstories.net, Vol. 8, #45, 2005; excerpted at: www.
          vancouverneon.com/page_q/only_seafoods.htm

p. 46:   John Mackie, "So long to
          another Vancouver icon: The
          Only Sea Food neon sign
          hauled away," *Vancouver Sun*,
          April 7, 2010: www.vancou-
          versun.com/long+another+
          Vancouver+icon+Only+
          Food+neon+sign+hauled+
          away/2774918/story.html

p. 46:   Giorgio Agamben, *L'usage*, vii.

p. 47:   In the footnote: Montaigne, *Essais*, II, XXXII (not I, XIV as in Agamben).

p. 47:   "Appuntamento a ora insolita" *The Selected Poetry and Prose of Vittorio Sereni: A Bilingual Edition*, transl. Marcus Perryman and Peter Robinson. Chicago: University of Chicago Press, 2008, 140. (Transl. of poem title in the current book is by the author.)

p. 54:   Judith Butler, *Notes*, 150.

p. 54:   Giorgio Agamben, *L'usage*, 51.

p. 55:   Giorgio Agamben, *L'usage*, 58. Translated by the author.

p. 59:   On Nick's Spaghetti House: www.facebook.com/matt.camozzi1/activity/10155857565685054

p. 60:   On Lazara Press, a progressive publishing house in Vancouver: http://lazarapress.ca

p. 62:   Review of Nick's: www.yelp.ca/biz/nicks-spaghetti-house-vancouver

p. 68:   Harold Ferdinand Joseph Moure started basic army training at No. 31 Cdn Army Training Centre in Cornwall, Ontario (which operated from 1940–44) where that first autumn the recruits may have slept in tents. There Harold contracted TB. He died March 16, 1952 of "monocytic leukemia and pulmonary tuberculosis," according to the post-mortem at the Ottawa Civic Hospital quoted April 29 by Dick Mouré in a letter to the author's father. The author still has Harold's stamp collection, kept by her father for 61 years until his own death. One photo of the camp has been found, and it does not picture tents. The author has a copy of an envelope addressed by his mother to Harold at the army camp, dated December 1940.

p. 69:   Clara Raina Flannigan & Anne Raina, *Clara's Rib: A True Story of a Young Girl Growing Up in a Tuberculosis Hospital*, 2010. www.anneraina.ca/purchase.php

p. 69:   John Curry, "Story of former Royal Ottawa Sanatorium told through experience of one family," *Stittsville News*, April 19, 2016. www.ottawacommunitynews.com/news-story/6501479-story-of-former-royal-ottawa-sanatorium-told-through-experience-of-one-family

p. 71:   On the Hildon Hotel: www.historicplaces.ca/en/rep-reg/place-lieu.aspx?id=8561

p. 72:   Image of hotel roof and sky are from the collection of Toots, and it cannot be determined now if it is really from Google Street View or was manipulated to look that way.

p. 73:   On The Bourbon: www.yelp.ca/biz/the-bourbon-vancouver

p. 75:   Closed Canadian Parks, on Belmont Park: www.cec.chebucto.org/ClosPark/Belmont.html

Some of Toots's words about the park could have been echoed from other sites, which I have tried hard to find. Any new information will be credited in future editions.

p. 76:   Giorgio Agamben, *L'usage*, first chapter.

p. 78:   Quote on the Décarie as scar is from the *Southern Décarie Design Brief* by The Advanced Urban Lab, Urban Studies Programme, Concordia University, 2002. Ed. Pierre Gauthier. www.concordia.ca/content/dam/artsci/geography-planning-environment/docs/student-projects/SouthernDecarie_DesignBrief.pdf

p. 79:   Image of the former Greek Village restaurant from the collection of Toots, possibly from Google Street View. Just in case, Google and the Google logo are registered trademarks of Google Inc. Such images, it seems, can only be embedded as code and not used as photos, so that Google can remove them from everywhere on the Internet if they receive a removal request. Sorry, Google, but it is for commentary purposes and cannot be replaced by any other image. Upon request, it will be removed from future editions.

On the history of the Greek Village restaurant, from Gerry Bellett, "Bardell paints a brighter future for Vancouver schoolchildren," *Vancouver Sun*, 22 November 2011, reprinted in *Läänekaare Postipoiss* No. 4, December 8, 2011. (Newsletter of the Vancouver Estonian Society). www.vesbc.com/documents/lp227.pdf

p. 80:   On Minto Village in Montréal: www.coolopolis.blogspot. ca/2013/03/minto-village-putting-face-to.html

p. 85:   Sandra Thomas, "Plaza 500 Hotel subject of growing list of lawsuits," *Vancouver Courier*, January 29, 2013. www.vancourier.com/ news/plaza-500-hotel-subject-of-growing-list-of-lawsuits-1.383223 . As of mid-2016, the building was to be completely rebuilt as rental housing, with a full-time concierge, pet-friendly floors, and with bicycle lockers as well as parking, with studio suites starting at $1750 per month. www.plaza500.com/building

p. 90:   Giorgio Agamben, *The Time That Remains: A Commentary on the Letter to the Romans*, trans. Patricia Dailey. Stanford CA: Stanford University Press, 2005, 40.

p. 90:   *Pierrot à Montréal*, dir. Donald Ginsberg, National Film Board of Canada, 1957, 30 min, view at www.nfb.ca/film/ pierrot_in_montreal

p. 90:   Photo from *Pierrot in Montréal* ©1957 National Film Board of Canada. All rights reserved. Used by permission.

p. 93:   Claude Poirier, "Le *pâté chinois*: le caviar des jours ordinaires," in *Le Trésor de la langue française*, XXV, Québec City: Université Laval, #70, May 1988. Our author mistakenly conflated the title of the newsletter with the article. www.tlfq.ulaval.ca/pub/pdf/H-25.pdf

p. 93: Fabien Deglise, "Le noble pâté," *Le Devoir*, December 15, 2007. www.ledevoir.com/plaisirs/alimentation/168722/le-noble-pate

p. 94: On *Take 30*: www.wikipedia.org/wiki/Take_30

p. 94: On Jehane Benoît: www.wikipedia.org/wiki/Jehane_Benoît

p. 95: On beef kidney: www.smithmeadows.com/kidney-recipes; www.livestrong.com/article/510033-how-to-prepare-beef-kidney

p. 99: *The Best of Dean Martin* was released in Duophonic Stereo by Capitol Records as DT–2106 in 1966, with these tracks:

1. That's Amore (Harry Warren, Jack Brooks) 3:07
2. You're Nobody 'Til Somebody Loves You (Russ Morgan, Larry Stock, James Cavanaugh) 2:13
3. Volare (Domenico Modugno, Franco Migliacci, Mitchell Parish) 3:00
4. It's Easy to Remember (And So Hard to Forget) (Richard Rodgers, Lorenz Hart) 3:16
5. Sway (Pablo Beltrán Ruiz, Norman Gimbel) 2:43
6. Return to Me (Ritorna-Me) (Carmen Lombardo, Danny Di Minno, English words added by Dan Hartman, Charlie Midnight) 2:25
7. Memories Are Made of This (Terry Gilkyson, Richard Dehr, Frank Miller) 2:17
8. June in January (Ralph Rainger, Leo Robin) 2:49
9. Come Back to Sorrento (Torna a Surriento) (Ernesto De Curtis, Claude Aveling) 3:14
10. Just in Time (Jule Styne, Betty Comden, Adolph Green) 2:14
11. I'm Yours (Johnny Green, E.Y. Harburg) 3:16
12. Hey, Brother, Pour the Wine (Ross Bagdasarian, Sr.) 2:53

All songs mentioned by title on p. 93–94 are from this album. No lyrics are included for copyright reasons, but readers can find the songs on YouTube.

The image of the antique store window with most of the album cover visible: the album cover is in the public domain in Canada as it was copyright by a corporation in 1966. In the USA, it is copyright Capitol Records, used here under fair use guidelines, considering:

1)   the entire image is needed to identify the product, properly convey the meaning and branding in the text, and avoid misrepresenting the image.

2)   the image is of sufficient resolution for commentary and identification but too low to permit pirate versions or other uses that would compete with the commercial purpose of the original artwork.

3)   the image is used for identification in the context of critical commentary and makes a significant contribution to the reader's understanding, which could not practically be conveyed by words alone. Use does not compete with the purposes of the original artwork, namely the provision of graphic design to music concerns so as to market music to the public.

4)   as musical cover art, the image is not replaceable by free content; any other image that shows the packaging would also be copyrighted, and any version not true to the original would be inadequate for identification or commentary.

p. 101:   On *The Dean Martin Show*: www.wikipedia.org/wiki/The_Dean_Martin_Show

p. 102:   « L'expérience des travailleurs de l'Abitibi, » in *Chantier politique*, #2, September 24, 2013. www.pmlq.qc.ca/Chantiers Politiques2013/CP01002.HTM

p. 103:   Judith Butler, *Notes*, 119.

p. 104:   Judith Butler, *Notes*, 120.

p. 104:   On chiasmus: www.wikipedia.org/wiki/Chiasmus

p. 108:   The hotel with the shuffleboard whose name Toots can't remember may have been the Metropole, at 320 Abbott Street. The photo on this page from 1978 rings a bell: https://changingvancouver.word press. com/tag/travellers-hotel/. The Metropole is still an SRO hotel today.

p. 109:   Judith Butler, *Notes*, 122.

p. 110:   Giorgio Agamben, *Means Without Ends: Notes on Politics*.
          Trans. Vincenzo Binetti and Cesare Casarino, Minneapolis MN:
          University of Minnesota Press, 2000, 3-4.

p. 110:   Mary Elizabeth Raina, *We Have Written: A True Story About
          Our Struggle to Maintain Dignity in the Face of Oppression*. Self-pub-
          lished, 1976, 1990. Available from Amazon.

p. 112:   Church and State had long turned their faces from the Abitib-
          iwinnik; no wonder they were not asked. This Algonquin-speaking
          nation, today at Pikogan near Amos, was given no reserve under
          Treaty 9 in 1906, nor were they even signatories as they lived on the
          Québec side and Québec refused to participate in Treaty 9, thus
          their traditional territory was never ceded. In 1958, the Abitibiwinni
          Nation was finally able to get the Indian agent to buy land with their
          own money for a reserve, to provide one small safe place to settle.
          Their semi-nomadic traditional lifestyle based at Apitipik Point on
          Lake Abitibi had long been crushed by colonization, mining, and
          the collapse of the fur trade. Only in the 1990s did Québec begin to
          sign agreements with the Abitibiwinnik. See Marie-Pierre Bousquet,
          "From Passive Consumers to Entrepreneurs: Building A Political
          Context for Economic Development in an Anishinabe Community
          in Québec," in Katia Iankova, Azizul Hassan, Rachel L'Abbé, ed.
          *Indigenous People and Economic Development: An International
          Perspective*. NY and London: Routledge, 2016. 97-109.

p. 113:   Quote on Jules Michaud from *Plan d'urbanisme : Municipalité
          de Saint-Marc-de-Figuery*, Février 2015, by André Labbé, conseiller
          en urbanisme. Trans. by the author. www.municipalites-du-quebec.
          org/municipalites/saint-marc-de-figuery/banque/215.pdf

p. 114:   On the Spirit Lake internment camp: www.campspiritlake.ca/
          Main.aspx?PageName=Accueil

p. 114:   On the Internment of Persons of Ukrainian Origin Recognition
          Act: http://laws.justice.gc.ca/eng/acts/I-20.8/page-1.html

p. 116:   *L'Abitibi, Une des plus belles régions agricoles de la Province de Québec: le témoignage d'un curé*, by M. L'abbé Beauchamp. Québec City: Ministère de la colonisation, des mines et des Pêcheries de la Province de Quebec, 1923.

www.collections.banq.qc.ca/bitstream/52327/2023362/1/1969.pdf

Also there is this: *Guide du colon*, 1944: www.ourroots.ca/toc. aspx?id=12071

p. 117:   Quote is from Marcotte, J.-Sam., *Rapport du Service du retour a la terre*, Rapport général du Ministère de la Colonisation, de la Chasse et des Pêcheries de la province de Québec pour 1933, Documents de la session, vol. 67, #2, 1934, pp. 80-90, p.86, cited in Maurice Asselin, *La colonisation de l'Abitibi, un projet géopolitique*. Travaux de recherches No. 4, Cahiers du Département d'histoire et de géographie. Rouyn QC: Collège de l'Abitibi, November 1982, 118. www. depositum.uqat.ca/422/1/cahierhist4.pdf

p. 118:   On Caen: www.wikipedia.org/wiki/Caen

p. 119:   Rainer Maria Rilke. *Letters to a Young Poet*. Trans. Stephen Mitchell. NY: Vintage Books, 1986, 78-79.

Or see: www.carrothers.com/rilke_main.htm

p. 124:   Photos from here onward, excepting the bottom of page 126 and page 132, are from the collection of the author.

p. 127:   The poem on this page is reprinted with the permission of the author. The book is out of print but still under copyright.

p. 132:   Photo by jmv, used under CC BY 2.0.

Remerciements

In January, 2016 when this text was complete, the seven days over, I knew it was not meant for publication. It was nobody's business but mine. Yet the traces of the little man could not reside only with me, outside of me, in words. There are no words until there is a reader.

I decided to make a small book on my own, and share it with fifteen people. If fifteen people read it, it would mean that he did have a funeral and that fifteen people came. It would be enough, for he was a modest man. I just didn't want him to disappear.

Many of those who read the little man's small book, by Toots, convinced me that the work had value, and should be published for others to read. I waited until the first year of mourning was over, and felt ready to listen to them.

My deepest thanks to Lou, Peter, Meredith, Colette, Jean-Antonin in memory, Chantal, Lisa, Jean-Philippe, Belén, Kim, Angela, George, Marianne, Rolf, Norma, Oana, and Karis for your words, and for letting me share Paul Émile Savard with you. Thanks to Pam too, whose simple email, on the day after the phone call from Betty, encouraged me to keep writing. Thanks to Loreen, my childhood friend, who also read it and wrote me. A few other people read it silently. And to Aaron, thanks, for tweeting his appreciation last December. The love you have shown this work then and now does mean the world to me.

Erín Moure
on behalf of Toots
September 28, 2017